Is Your Home Making You Sick?

by Dr Peter Dingle

ISBN: 978-0-9806131-0-0

Editor: Conna Craig
Cover: Mark Welsh
Illustrations: Jon Rowdon
Desktop: Gayle Chappell

Preface

In 1999 I wrote a small book called Sick Homes 1 about toxic chemicals in homes, and in 2002 I wrote the sequel Sick Homes 2 about dust, microbes and cleaning. Now, 25,000 copies of each book later, I have decided to write this update and fill some of the gaps on the science of sick homes.

Part One of this book introduces the concept of unclean air and discusses the major reasons it is a problem as well as the general health implications of indoor air pollutants (IAPs). It also covers why children and certain other groups are more susceptible to toxins.

Part Two is focused on chemicals that cause indoor air pollution. We take these chemicals into our homes, often with the mistaken belief that they will help us create a better and cleaner indoor environment. This part of the book will also focus on the many common materials in our homes that pollute our indoor air by "gassing off" hazardous chemicals.

Part Three is about combustion products, from the gases coming from unflued heaters and cookers to tobacco smoke and car exhaust pipes, particularly associated with garages attached to homes.

Part Four deals with a related issue—the tiny particles of dust that collect in our homes and greatly affect our health. The focus of this part of the book is the potential hazard of that dust, including the components of its microscopic particles, biological contaminants (such as bacteria, mould and dust mites) and our cleaning practices and equipment. Dust and our methods of cleaning are things we often take for granted. Dust is everywhere and everyone knows how to vacuum! We may have never given dust a great deal of thought until finding we are ill without a readily identifiable cause. In actuality, few people know much about real dust elimination or, as I prefer to describe it, the science of cleaning.

Part Five introduces the dangers of radiation. Exposure to radiation is associated with an increased risk of cancer. The potential harm of electromagnetic radiation from mobile phones and power lines continues to be the subject of much controversy.

Part Six covers Sick Building Syndrome, including its causes and how it affects the health of many people who work in office buildings that are toxic.

Finally, in the conclusion I offer a few thoughts about how you and your family can achieve better health, wherever you live and work.

This book will change your attitudes to many things around your home. I'll show you that with a few simple modifications you can easily improve the health status of your home, your wellbeing and that of your family. And this doesn't mean you need to become a paranoid, compulsive, obsessive cleaner. In many cases, it will actually mean doing less cleaning, just doing it better. Doesn't that sound nice!

Dr Peter Dingle,
2009

CONTENTS
Part One

ACKNOWLEDGEMENTS

I would like to thank all my students who helped me compile this information over the years from my undergraduate students particularly Carla Webster and Dale Parsonage, and my research students Dr Peter Franklin, Rita Tan, Joanne Nastov, Peter Tapsell, Andre Maynard, Ross Pontin, Adrian Statico, Dr Peter Kemp, Jane Jones, Kevin White and Cedric Cheong.

I would like to give a special thanks to my mum, Irene Dingle who instilled all the values that I have and at 86 is still active and inspirational to me. I would also like to thank all the people who have motivated me over the years and put up with my strange work habits; especially Martine, my beautiful wife, for her encouragement, and our kids Ellie, Matthew and Melissa for their enthusiasm and for keeping me in touch with reality.

A special thanks to Jon Rowdon for the fantastic graphics in every one of my books. They really add such a positive dimension to the books. For Gayle Chappell who sets out my books to make them so readable. To Conna Craige for her edits that tidy up so much of my sloppy writing and Mark Welsh for the cover. It is a great team.

Ultimately, I would like to say a big thank you to all the public who support me in what I do. For without your support we could not affect the change necessary to keep governments and companies accountable and the public empowered with the truth.

PART ONE

Chapter 1. Indoor Air and Health

Indoor air pollution has become an increasingly important public health issue. While people are becoming more concerned about outdoor air pollution with haze and smog forming over most of our cities, many people do not stop to think that the average person spends 80 to 90 percent of his or her time indoors - at home, at work, in the car or at school.

Not only do we spend more of our time indoors than ever before, but also the construction of modern buildings has led to our increased exposure to microscopic dust, combustion gases, biological indoor air pollutants, synthetic chemicals and electromagnetic radiation. Today's buildings are generally more airtight—with double brick walls, aluminium window frames, plastic window seals and insulation—than the buildings of decades ago. Ceilings are lower and the use of concrete slabs rather than wooden flooring creates an impervious floor surface. We have successfully made our homes and offices snug against the outside environment but this has resulted in low air exchange and poor ventilation. In some cases, an ideal environment has been created for dust to accumulate and for certain microorganisms to flourish. These factors and the prevalence of air conditioning (which recycles air, but does not clean it) contribute significantly to higher concentrations of indoor contaminants. The air-tightness of our homes is exacerbated by our reluctance to open doors and windows to let in some "fresh" outdoor air. It is not uncommon to find homes with all windows kept closed and air conditioning running nearly around the clock, constantly recycling stale air.

The air exchange rate between the outside air and the indoor air of homes is 10 times lower than it was about 30 years ago. Although current building codes are required in commercial buildings for improved ventilation along with energy conservation, nothing has changed for homes, where indoor air problems persist and in many cases are getting worse.

In the outdoor environment, there are risk limits imposed on pollutants yet those "safe" pollution levels are often exceeded for certain pollutants when we are indoors. In office buildings the need to find more space results in the partitioning of rooms. This blocks the normal airflow and produces pockets of "dead air;" these pockets can have severe indoor pollution problems.

This book is really about home health, which, believe it or not, is a very political and emotional area. We may think that we clean our homes efficiently, but science is now showing us that we often leave our homes dirtier or more polluted after cleaning than when we started. (Some people may find their noses a bit out of joint after reading criticisms of their general cleaning practices. For that we apologise.) However, everyone we spoke to said this book had to be written and agreed enthusiastically with its principles. We hope to stimulate you to think about home hygiene and to clean, not simply for aesthetics or for social reasons, as when someone's coming to dinner, but for health.

For many years I have been saying that the most important health professionals in the world are the people who look after our homes, including the people who clean them. Think about that for a moment. Our modern medical system is largely reactive in response, treating the symptoms of established disease or dysfunction but not the actual causes. Home health and cleaning is a fundamental and essential preventative measure that helps to protect us from disease. History has demonstrated, especially in the great plagues that beset Europe in the 1600s, that the most important causes of living longer and healthier lives are based on improved hygiene: proper waste elimination and treatment, cleaner water, food and living environments. Other than the role of antibiotics and certain vaccinations, medicine has played a role secondary to hygiene.

This raises home health and domestic cleaning to a new status. Far from being seen as a household chore of nominal importance, it can be regarded as a valuable and important practice for good health.

Your upper body is, in essence, a sponge for air. It is specifically designed for breathing. The moist, delicate membranes of the tiny grape-like bunches of air sacs (alveoli) in your lungs provide a cellular surface area as large as a tennis court. This large area is necessary for an efficient exchange of gases. Oxygen passes over the membranes into the bloodstream and in return the lungs take up the blood's burden of carbon dioxide. The alveoli are lined with a filmy surface of mucous, which not only encourages gas exchange but also acts as a trap for particles and contaminants which have managed to slip by your body's earlier defence systems in your nose, upper nasal passage and throat. In the alveoli, macrophages, which are your immune system's cellular rubbish collectors, engulf the foreign intruders and render them harmless.

If your lungs are a uniquely designed sponge for air, they are also a sponge for the contaminants that manage to evade all of your respiratory system's defences. These contaminants are inhaled as invisible and frequently odourless chemical and physical compounds. They may be the products of car exhaust or factory emissions, or the gases emitted from seemingly benign household products such as glues, paints, plastics, cleaning products, gas stoves and heaters, kerosene heaters, laminated wood products, furniture and personal products (such as deodorants and hair spray). Even the contaminants tracked into your home on the soles of your shoes can enter deep into your lungs. Because many contaminants are in a gaseous form or are suspended in the air as ultra-fine particles, they too pass through the thin membranes of your lungs into your bloodstream. From there they circulate throughout your body to your brain, liver, kidneys and other organs. Only 30 percent of the contaminants inhaled are ever exhaled; the remaining 70 percent must be broken down by your liver or otherwise dealt with by your body.

The resting adult breathes 10,000 to 20,000 litres of air daily. Every day we breathe a largely unknown and unmeasurable cocktail of various chemicals in a gaseous or particulate form. Sometimes these emissions are quite obvious in their odour and immediate effects. We may be alerted by a strong smell or may suffer irritation of our eyes, nose and throat or experience headaches or nausea. More often than not, however, there is no alerting odour or noticeable physical reaction and, as a result, we don't take steps to avoid the exposure. In some cases we may even relate the smell to pleasant and positive perceptions, such as a new house or carpet, not realising that over a long period this exposure may affect our health. In other instances we simply become complacent about the stuffy or musty odour, not realising that the source is a toxic mould.

Respiratory disease

The cause of certain respiratory problems is being increasingly linked to environmental pollutants and, in particular, to the quality of the air we breathe. Respiratory disease ranks third as a leading cause of death in most developed countries and ranks sixth amongst disabilities leading to premature retirement. The group of chronic obstructive pulmonary diseases—including conditions such as bronchiolitis, chronic bronchitis and emphysema—are amongst the most common disabling respiratory diseases in most Western nations. Air contaminants that cause respiratory disease include viruses and bacteria, moulds, nitrogen dioxide, carbon monoxide, volatile organic compounds (VOCs), formaldehyde and various particulates.

The term "allergy" refers to the development of a heightened immune response to a particular substance or substances. The allergic individual's immune system reacts to a commonly occurring substance, such as pollen, as if it were toxic or harmful and then produces antibodies to fight it. The offending substance is called an "allergen" (also known as an "antigen"). Allergies occur when the immune system mistakes a harmless substance for an infectious one and begins to attack it. The immune system acts to release histamine into the blood and antibodies from cells and organs to fight the perceived infection. Allergens may be inhaled (e.g., airborne particles such as pollens or dust mite faeces) ingested (e.g., foods such as strawberries, shellfish or certain medications) or simply come into contact with the skin (e.g., plants such as grevillea or some of the chemicals found in hair dyes, face creams, shampoos and mascara). An allergic reaction may spread rapidly beyond the site of allergen contact and in cases of extreme reaction (such as allergy to bee venom or peanuts) may cause anaphylactic shock and death.

The allergic reaction is caused by a hypersensitive immune response: the immunoglobulin E (Ig-E, a special protein with antibody activity which is found in the blood serum) binds with the allergen (the substance which the immune system has identified as being a threat). The Ig-E then releases chemicals that produce an over-protective reaction in the body: inflammation, swelling, increased secretions from the mucous membranes and the skin, muscle spasm and other allergic symptoms. Asthma, contact dermatitis and hives are the result of such responses. People with sensitivity to one substance are more likely to develop multiple allergies. People with asthma usually have elevated levels of Ig-E antibodies. New research on Ig-E levels in the blood has shown that it is the only reliable indicator of the presence of allergies. Although skin prick tests are still used they are at best a general indicator, not conclusive and sometimes misleading.

Inhaled allergens can provoke an immune response in the upper and lower respiratory tract, the eyes and the skin. Conditions such as asthma, chronic allergic rhinitis, sinusitis and hay fever all involve inflammation and overactivity of the mucous membranes and may be associated with eczema and other forms of allergy-related dermatitis. The severity of the reaction varies with each person's sensitivity and the allergen involved. In the instance of inhaled allergens, the size of the particle determines its ability to penetrate the lungs. The particles that can penetrate the respiratory system most deeply will produce an immune reaction in the lower respiratory tract, such as asthma. Larger particles deposited in the upper respiratory tract are thought to produce conditions such as rhinitis and sinusitis.

Asthma

The word "asthma" is derived from Greek, meaning panting. Asthma is characterised by attacks of shortness of breath and difficulty breathing, accompanied by wheezing. The wheezy breathing of asthmatics is due to spasms in the smooth muscle of the bronchial tubes and the inflammation of their mucous membranes. Asthma may occur in childhood, young adulthood or middle age. It occurs among all races and shows no preference for gender. Chronic asthma, if not properly treated, can cause emphysema. In countries such as the USA, Australia, New Zealand, the UK and parts of Europe, asthma affects one in 10 adults and as many as one in four children. The incidence of this disease has increased dramatically over the past five decades but may be reaching a plateau. In Australia, approximately 2.2 million people are clinically diagnosed with the condition; each year hundreds of people die from asthma attacks. It is the most widespread chronic illness in our community.

An asthma attack is the main symptom of the disease. The asthmatic usually suffers these at night, waking with breathlessness and wheezing and experiencing a sense of suffocation as the muscles surrounding the bronchi and bronchioles contract, decreasing the internal diameter of these airways. The chest feels tight and constricted and is noticeably distended. This restriction and spasm make it harder for the asthmatic to push the air out of his or her lungs. The gasping effort to breathe often results in a state of panic and is frightening and traumatic for both the asthmatic and his or her family. The last stage of the attack is reached after half an hour to several hours: violent coughing that brings up copious amounts of very thick, tenacious mucous. This final paroxysm brings relief, yet the sufferer is left exhausted and aching. Severe attacks may last for days and usually require hospitalisation.

Not all asthma attacks are the same. They can vary from being mild and short lasting to fatal. The frequency varies between individuals, depending upon the trigger. Short-lived attacks can be recurrent over days or even weeks. They commonly occur during the night, during winter or in rainy seasons when humidity is high.

Despite the number of people affected by asthma, the cause of the disease is still not known with certainty, although recent science suggests the rate correlates to early childhood diet and gut health. We do know that there are many factors that can predispose a person to developing asthma. Increased exposure to allergens and indoor air pollutants, such as formaldehyde and tobacco smoke, are important risk factors. In addition, there are probable links to lifestyle. It is also possible that the lack of exposure to infections in early life, certain vaccinations and even some medications may contribute to the development of the disease.

The increase in allergic disease seems to have something to do with our Western lifestyle because it happens in the West; people who move from developing countries to First World environments seem to get more asthma.

The allergic reactions that are caused by the faeces of mites, organic dust, pollen, animal fur and other dust-related compounds all cause similar health symptoms. Chemical compounds such as formaldehyde, tobacco smoke and nitrogen dioxide can induce asthma and asthmatic attacks. Recent research has shown that these gaseous pollutants can increase an individual's sensitivity to allergens. It is also possible that air pollutants may interact with airborne allergens and increase their potency and effects. They may have a direct toxic effect on the cells lining our airways, causing inflammation and increasing the cells' permeability to other pollutants.

Smoking and asthma

Smoke can cause asthma attacks in diagnosed asthmatics and it may be a primary cause of the disease. A strong link has been found between the number of cigarettes smoked by parents and the risk of their children developing wheezing bronchitis and/or asthma. All the literature we have studied confirms that smoking can cause asthma attacks and is detrimental to asthmatics.

Studies have shown that smokers tend to have higher immunoglobulin E levels than non-smokers. This suggests that a smoker's immune system becomes sensitised to an antigen and that the smoker will be more susceptible to developing an allergic reaction to that substance. While I would encourage anyone who smokes to stop for their own health, I must emphasize that smoking in the car or home where there are children or non-smokers is unacceptable. The detrimental health effects of tobacco smoke are clearly documented and the chemicals released from the burning cigarette stay in the indoor air of a car or home for many hours.

Causes of allergies and asthma: a dietary link

Despite 40 years of research on indoor air pollution, there is very little evidence to suggest that it causes asthma. It is a major trigger to asthma attacks but it does not appear to cause asthma except at very high levels. Allergies generally develop in early childhood with a median age of 24 months at onset. Underlying factors responsible for the increase in allergies and atopic disorders may include bottle-feeding, early introduction of solid foods and imbalance in the immune system (T helper development in favour of Th2 over Th1 cells) and exposure to high levels of allergens.

One hypothesis that has growing support is the "hygiene hypothesis," also referred to as "exaggerated hygiene." This hypothesis suggests that little or no exposure to bacteria and viruses during a critical period of infancy can lead to an imbalance in the immune system and result in diseases such as asthma, especially in high-risk groups such as children with parents who have asthma. Researchers theorize that when infants are exposed to germs early on, their immune systems are pushed to go in an "infection-fighting direction." Without this push, the immune system's shift to infection fighting is delayed and it becomes more likely to overreact to allergens - including dust, mould, and other environmental elements such as food molecules - that most people can tolerate.

More likely it is the conditions that lead to gut dysbiosis - imbalances in the intestinal flora - such as use of antibiotics by pregnant mothers and Caesarean births in particular, that contribute to the increase in allergies, including peanut and other food allergies. We are, quite literally, too clean inside.

The gut is a dynamic living organ in the body that is in constant contact and communication with its surrounding media. The mucous membrane absorbs and assimilates foods and serves as a barrier to pathogens and other foreign chemicals and particles (antigens). Optimal functioning of the gut relies on good intestinal integrity. When this integrity is compromised, the permeability of the gut may be altered; little gaps appear and gut function erodes. Two major factors that determine the integrity of the gut are health of the gut lining (the mucosa) and a balanced bacterial population.

The human gut is the natural habitat for a large and dynamic bacterial community with more than one hundred trillion bacteria consisting of hundreds of different species. The highest amount, 30 to 50 percent of the bacteria including more than 400 species, is in the large intestine; these bacteria affect the large intestine's cell biology, structure and balance.

Major functions of the gut bacteria include: metabolic activities that result in improved nutrition through the breakdown of food into usable energy; important feeding effects on the gut lining; immune structure and function; and protection of the colonised host against invasion by "alien" microbes. The gut bacteria also help manage gut physiology, particularly barrier integrity.

The gut lining (mucosa) is composed of close fitting, thin and semi-permeable (epithelial) cells separated by tight junctures. When the intestinal mucosa (cells including enterocytes and colonocytes) is disrupted, the permeability may increase, allowing larger particles, bacteria, undigested foods or toxins to cross the barrier into the blood... causing an immune reaction and a subsequent allergy.

Unlike most other cells in the body, which get their energy and nutrients from the blood supply, more than 50 percent of the energy needs of the small intestine and more than 80 percent of the energy of the large intestine (where most of the bacteria are) come directly from the food in the gut. The preferred foods of these cells are short-chain fatty acids like butyrate, acetate and propionate. These are derived from the metabolism of indigestible carbohydrates in dietary fibre by beneficial gut bacteria, especially Bifidobacteria (which are at their highest concentration during breast feeding). The bacteria in the gut literally create the "food" for the gut lining.

Any change in the relative proportions of the different bacteria alters the nutrients subsequently available for the digestive tract and its health. If the right food is not available, the cells can literally get sick and starve. Pathogenic bacteria or other microorganisms that colonise in the gut can also cause damage to the GI mucosa by releasing toxins. Fortunately, the good gut bacteria help to keep the pathogenic bacteria in check.

About 80 percent of the body's immune system is localized around the gastrointestinal tract. Experimental data and clinical studies have shown that the immune system of infants can be stimulated by the intestinal bacteria, with specific prebiotics and probiotics being shown to promote mucosal immunologic maturation in infants. The first months of life and up to two years of age represent a critical period for the maturation of the infant's immune system and, thus, a window of opportunity for measures to improve immune function and reduce the risk of disease.

Numerous recent studies including blinded placebo-controlled studies (the gold standard of clinical studies) have supported these findings. In one study, infants at risk of developing atopy who received special probiotics during the first six months of life had a fifty percent reduction in atopic dermatitis after two years compared to the control group. The intake of probiotic-supplemented yoghurt reduced Japanese cedar pollinosis symptoms in infants. Administration of the probiotics at the time of introduction of cow's milk in the infants' diets resulted in higher tolerance to cow's milk. The intake of probiotics showed a small reduction in the days of illness, respiratory tract infections and gastrointestinal disorders and improved the response to Hib immunization in six-month-old infants. The beneficial effect of prebiotics (oligosaccharides) has also been demonstrated in a high-risk population of infants.

A number of studies have now shown no adverse effects associated with probiotic use in infants as young as neonates, even in highly susceptible groups.

The cause of the problem

Possible factors contributing to disruption of healthy gut bacteria, gut dysbiosis and an increased risk of developing allergies as an infant include:

- Antibiotics given to the mother or child;
- Caesarean birth;
- Preservatives such as antimicrobials; and
- Poor food such as dairy and wheat.

It is widely acknowledged that the use of broad-spectrum antibiotics has negative effects on intestinal integrity and may alter the balance between beneficial and pathogenic bacteria. This is especially important in children, for whom antibiotics are prescribed frequently. Even unborn children can experience these effects when expecting mothers receive antibiotics. Colonization of the infant's digestive tract occurs during the transition through the birthing canal, and gut dysbiosis may remain for up to twelve months after an initial disruption. Clinicians should therefore consider co-administration of probiotics with antibiotics.

Caesarean delivery alters the bacterial colonization of the newborn's gut for more than six months. The bacterial colonization normally occurs shortly after birth and may have a protective effect against the predisposition to asthma and allergies. A number of large studies have shown that Caesarean delivery is associated with wheezing and allergic sensitisation. The gastrointestinal tract of a healthy foetus is sterile. During the birth process and rapidly thereafter, microbes from the mother and the surrounding environment colonize the gastro-intestinal tract until a dense, complex microflora develops.

Diet is a major factor in maintaining a healthy human gastro-intestinal tract. In infants who are breast-fed, bifidobacteria constitute about 90 percent of their intestinal bacteria; however, this number is lower in bottle-fed infants and when infants' diets are changed to cow's milk and solid food. Foods with a high prebiotic potential such as vegetables, fruit and beans (legumes) will help maintain a healthy gut bacteria population.

"Occam's razor" is a basic premise of science and suggests that the simplest solution is the most effective. Unfortunately, in today's pharmacology-dominated medical industry, the simplest, most basic solutions are not always employed. The addition of probiotics to the diets of infants and pregnant mothers is a simple, easy and logical step now supported with a large amount of scientific evidence. And while colonisation in adults appears to be only short-lived, in infants it is stable for as long as six months and may persist for as long as 24 months.

This approach is cheap, easy to implement and has no negative side effects. The cost would be a mere fraction of the medical costs of one child who contracts a severe nut allergy. The added benefit is that we already know it will help in the reduction of other health issues such as asthma and gut-related problems.

For the children, this is a win-win approach to lifelong good health.

Chapter 4. Susceptible Groups

Some people are more likely to have problems with indoor air pollution than others, even when the amounts of contaminants present are seemingly quite low. Asthmatics have particular sensitivities. Any chemicals, gases or particulates that cause irritation of the respiratory system's mucous membranes will aggravate an asthmatic's condition.

Allergy prone people who already show sensitivity to a substance with reactions such as sinusitis, hay fever, atopic eczema and other forms of atopic dermatitis are likely to react with heightened sensitivity to indoor air pollution. They may experience an aggravation of their allergies or develop additional sensitivities. The increasing number of people who suffer from 21st century diseases such as chronic fatigue and multiple chemical sensitivities will also react to even very low levels of indoor pollution.

The elderly, especially those who are frail and infirm, are more likely than others to develop respiratory disorders. Pregnant women, who may themselves enjoy robust health, are at risk because some of these contaminants pass over the placenta to the foetus. People under stress are more at risk because their immune systems are often not functioning at optimum levels. Other factors determining susceptibility include gender, genetic makeup, pre-existing health conditions and predisposition to disease, as well as lifestyle considerations such as work, diet and exercise.

Chemicals and kids

There is little doubt that our kids have a greater susceptibility to toxic chemicals than we do. Every day we expose our children to hundreds of different chemicals in an array of household products and yet remain puzzled as to why they get sick and why the rates of childhood asthma, allergies and cancer are higher than ever.

There are many contributing factors that increase rates of childhood disease. These include very important considerations such as diet, lifestyle and attitude. I wish to draw your attention to your child's immediate environment, as it is the environment you provide in your home that will contribute greatly to either your child's enjoyment of good health or development of disease. Over the past 40 to 50 years we have increased the number of synthetic chemicals we use with virtually no careful thought as to how vulnerable children are to these chemicals or how little we know about the chemicals' subtle and cumulative toxic effects. We assume that because these chemicals are so easily available off the supermarket shelf, they must be safe to use. Wrong! Many of these chemicals are known to be toxic and few of them are extensively studied before they are put on the shelf, freely available to the general public. Furthermore, certain assumptions are made in the process of allowing these products to be generally available. One of these assumptions is that kids are simply smaller versions of adults. Scientific and medical studies show that this is not the case and that children are much more vulnerable than adults to chemical toxins and environmental pollutants.

The World Health Organisation has emphasized that infants and young children have different structural and functional characteristics than those of older children and adults. These characteristics are simply stages of normal growth and development but affect a child's vulnerability when exposed to chemicals. In March 2005, the US Environmental Protection Agency (US EPA) reiterated that children are more vulnerable to gene-damaging chemicals than are adults.

For the first time, the US EPA has tried to put a figure on how much more susceptible children are than adults. The organisation reported that children two years old and younger might be 10 times more vulnerable than adults to certain chemicals and that children between the ages of two and 16 might be three times more vulnerable to certain chemicals. This means that we need to make a huge shift in the way we regulate chemicals. It also means that, in some cases, chemicals to which kids are exposed in the home are up to 10 times too high in concentration. Oops!

Our regulators have made yet another mistake and while they will say there are no problems with the existing system and will defend it, along with the manufacturing industry, it will eventually be changed—it will just take 10 or 20 years for it to happen. I have seen this many times. It was argued for decades that low levels of lead were not a problem but in just two or three years all the regulations were changed in the reluctant recognition that even low levels were a major health concern for kids. The scientific proof of this was available 20 or even 30 years earlier with the US removing lead from petrol in 1972. Australian authorities sat on their hands until 1986.

Kids are more vulnerable to toxic chemicals because of certain behavioural and physiological characteristics that not only multiply their exposures to environmental toxins but also increase the effects of these chemicals. Physiological characteristics include rapid rates of growth, immature body systems and physiology, such as enzyme systems, as well as underdeveloped barriers that prevent toxins from being absorbed. Kids are particularly vulnerable to toxins during rapid periods of growth such as those that occur in utero, during the first 12 months of life and at puberty. A typical human infant increases in weight by about 200 percent and in length by 50 percent in his or her first 12 months. On average, the infant's brain is just over 30 percent of the weight of an adult brain at birth; the maximum number of neurons will be reached by age two but the brain will not structurally mature until the child is four to six years of age. The nervous system is not fully developed until adolescence. A fatty sheath called myelin protects the spinal cord and the peripheral nerves and the process of neural myelination is not complete until adolescence. As a result, a child's nervous system is at higher risk of damage from common household insecticides, heavy metals and solvents typically found in household products.

A child's brain is also vulnerable to toxins because of the immaturity of the blood-brain barrier, which is designed to protect the brain from toxins. Even in adults this barrier cannot protect the brain from many heavy metals and synthetic chemicals such as solvents and pesticides. In infants it is almost totally ineffective against most modern day chemicals. This dramatically increases the risk of both temporary and permanent damage to the brain. It's possible that early exposure to some chemicals may permanently reduce the effectiveness of the blood-brain barrier, allowing increased passage of toxins to the brain, and increasing a person's lifelong vulnerability to certain chemicals.

Children are also susceptible in other areas of their physiology. The many enzyme pathways that metabolise foreign compounds in the body take several years to develop and a child is at increased risk until he or she is fully mature. For example, infants have lower levels of the neurotransmitter cholinesterase, which helps to maintain the balance in the nervous system's communication channels. Many pesticides and the nicotine in tobacco smoke inactivate cholinesterase, allowing the stimulating neurotransmitter acetylcholine to remain and increase in concentration, causing overstimulation of the nervous system. Depressed levels of cholinesterase can cause irreversible damage. Chronic effects include weakness and malaise, headache and light-headedness and symptoms that mimic those of ADHD. While the pesticides may not accumulate to any significant degree, repeated exposures with the resultant cholinesterase-inhibiting effect can be a significant problem. Don't expose your children (or yourself) to pesticides—any of them. Even if claims are made as to their safety, they are not safe! The aerosol spraying method for household insect killing chemicals enables the toxins to penetrate deep into the lungs. You wouldn't expose your kids to tobacco smoke, so why pesticides? They are much more toxic.

Children's immature enzyme systems can also affect their ability to eliminate the environmental toxins to which they are exposed. The metabolic pathways and enzyme detoxification systems of infants and young children have, as compared to adults, reduced capacity for dealing with toxins. The major excretory organs in the human body (the liver and kidney) take some years to develop and become fully and efficiently functional. For example, the Phase I and II enzyme detoxification systems (stimulated in all the liver detox diets) are immature at birth and develop only gradually in infants. The immaturity of an infant's capacity for detoxification and elimination usually produces higher blood levels of toxins for longer periods in comparison to an adult, meaning the toxic chemical hangs around a lot longer in your kids' bodies, doing more damage.

In general, tissue and membrane barriers are more permeable in the early years of life to help with the demands of rapid development and growth. However, this also increases their capacity to absorb toxins. For example, absorption rates of heavy metals from the gastrointestinal tract in humans and other mammals are significantly higher in infancy compared to other ages. Lead is a well-known poison, causing irreversible neurological damage to the young, including a reduced IQ. Studies have shown that infants and young children absorb lead more efficiently via the gastrointestinal tract than adults. From 40 to 90 percent of an oral dose is absorbed by a child less than eight years of age, compared to 10 percent by an adult. Studies have also shown that retention of the absorbed dose is higher. While adults retain 10 percent of an ingested dose, 18 percent is retained by children and 32 percent retained by children under five years of age. Absorption through the skin is also higher in children, as their skin is more permeable and they have a greater surface area relative to body weight than adults.

Kids are also at increased risk from environmental carcinogens. In infants and children cells are dividing more rapidly. There is a greater probability of DNA mutation and cancerous growth being initiated. Studies have shown that one-day-old rats exposed to vinyl chloride developed a much higher incidence of cancers than rats exposed at eleven weeks of age. Early exposure to carcinogens also means there is more time for cancer to develop over a person's lifetime. Some cancers that develop in adults are a result of exposure to carcinogens in childhood. Reducing childhood exposure to these toxic chemicals will reduce the potential for cancers later in life.

Kids' behaviour

Aside from the physiological and biochemical reasons behind children's increased susceptibility to toxins, there are behavioural, cultural and sociological reasons as to why they are more at risk than adults.

Increased exposure of infants and kids occurs through both their food consumption and respiration. Kilogram for kilogram of body weight, children drink more fluids, eat more food and breathe more air than adults. Children ages one to five years, for example, eat three to four times more food per kilogram of body weight than the average adult. The types of food they eat also increase their exposure. In the first five to seven years of life, a child's diet is very limited. One study in the US estimated that children between one and five years of age consumed six times the amount of fruit consumed by women ages 22 to 30 and, in particular, 18 times more apple and apple products, including juices and purees. More recent estimates from studies in the US suggest that the intake of apples by infants expressed as a ratio of body weight may be up to 20 times higher than that for adults. These consumption rates mean that young children face a greater risk from residues such as pesticides and fungicides in fresh produce than do adults. This highlights the need to choose for our kids organic and biodynamic produce as often as possible.

Young children's play behaviour can be a potential source of exposure to toxic substances. Mouthing, whereby hands and objects are put into the mouth, has been shown to lead to significant ingestion of soil and dust. One study found average daily estimates of soil consumed by kids ranged from 25.3 to 81.3 mg/day and reported that this was consistent with results from other studies. This dramatically increases their risk of exposure to heavy metals and pesticides in the soil. This doesn't mean that you stop your children from playing outside. It does mean you shouldn't use any pesticides or toxic chemicals in the garden.

Other behaviour such as crawling and playing close to the ground can also contribute to higher exposure to many chemicals, as this is where many of the chemicals actually accumulate. Children's tendency to play around cars while the engine is running really highlights this. More than 4,000 chemicals spew from the exhaust pipes of cars. I often see kids playing around the car while parents are saying their farewells. For kids, who are closer to exhaust pipe height, it's a toxic game.

Kids also don't have the experience or know-how to reduce their exposure. Unlike adults who can relate a chemical smell to making them sick or causing an allergic reaction, young children have too little experience to make the connection and often lack the necessary verbal skills to express that connection. So they will continue to expose themselves to more of the toxin. We, as adults and parents, must provide the protection of a safe environment. And children are easily influenced by the conditioning of media advertising to use toxic chemicals such as deodorant spray cans or perfumes, or to consume junk foods with toxic food additives in them.

Research is proving the toxicity of these chemicals. Many studies, including some of our own research and other Australian studies, show that the higher the use of chemicals in the home, including cleaning chemicals and the use of spray cans and pesticides, the higher the incidence of childhood disease such as asthma and allergies. In a few years when the research is complete, it will also show an increase in the rates of cancer in children and adults.

It is also worth noting that domestic chemicals poison thousands of kids every year. Some of them are permanently damaged. Some children die. The fewer toxic chemicals you bring into your home, the safer it is for your children, you and our environment.

Chapter 5. Chemical Pollutants

We are introducing many new, synthetic chemicals into our homes, using them on our skin and hair and in our mouths and breathing them daily, yet we really do not know what impact they have on our health—or for that matter on the environment at large.

While it is recognised that lifestyle and dietary factors are contributing to the increase in cancers and chronic, degenerative diseases, there is also no doubt that chemicals—both synthetic and natural—are playing a role in making us sick. I have seen this proven through my research and the research of my students. Even more compellingly, I know this through the thousands of people I speak with every year who are suffering ill health due to chemical exposure. Most of these people are ill from exposure to what we accept as "normal," everyday chemicals in our homes.

Sources of chemical pollutants include direct use of chemical-based products like lacquers, varnishes, cleaning products and aerosol cans as well as off-gassing from materials. Off-gassing is a form of evaporation that occurs with solid materials. Many manufactured materials contain chemicals that are not stable and these are slowly released into the surrounding air.

Chemical indoor air pollutants that have been identified as causing health problems are formaldehyde and volatile organic compounds (VOCs) such as:

- Benzene
- Ethyl benzene
- Xylene
- Toluene
- N-undecane
- N-dodecane
- Chloroform
- Trichloroethane
- Trichloroethylene
- Styrene
- Methyl acetate

The dangers of chemical cocktails are exacerbated by the fact that an ever-increasing number of chemicals are continually introduced into the marketplace. Many of them have not been well-studied and there is scant toxicological information available about their effects. There is even less information available on some of the older chemicals which have been around for years.

The next chapters will identify some of the common household and office products that produce chemical vapours injurious to your health and will provide some solutions to minimise your exposure.

Chapter 6. Formaldehyde

Perhaps the best known of the indoor air pollutants and the most studied is formaldehyde, a very simple chemical made up of two hydrogen, one carbon and one oxygen atom. Its simple structure and diverse properties have led it to be widely used in many products. Formaldehyde is specifically used for its preservative and microbial properties; in addition, when mixed with certain other products it makes excellent glue. As a result, formaldehyde is very widely used in manufacturing and is a pollutant found in all indoor environments.

Toxic effects

Formaldehyde is commonly linked with Sick Building Syndrome (SBS) and poor indoor air quality in new and renovated buildings. Its high toxicity results in adverse health effects at low concentrations. Exposure causes irritation of the eyes, skin and respiratory tract, wheezing, nausea, coughing, dizziness and lethargy at levels as low as 50 parts per billion (ppb). It has also been associated with aggravation of asthma, emphysema and hay fever as well as other allergies. Formaldehyde is currently considered a potential carcinogen to humans.

As a preservative and anti-microbial, formaldehyde has been added to personal care products such as soaps, cosmetics and shampoos and also to cleaning products and clothes. This is a major concern because it is a strong skin irritant. Use of formaldehyde-containing products can cause severe skin irritation and rashes. It is slowly being removed from these products as people become more informed and look for safer alternatives to this dangerous chemical.

Sources of formaldehyde

The main sources of formaldehyde in the indoor air are pressed wood products such as particleboard and plywood. The use of these products is increasing in homes as a substitute for solid timber, particularly in kitchen and bathroom benches and shelving and most built-in furniture. Paints, lacquers, varnishes and glues can also be a significant short-term source of formaldehyde. Recently a large number of material furnishings from curtains to blankets to children's toys have been brought in from China and have been discovered to have extremely high levels of formaldehyde.

Indoor air quality decreases dramatically when new homes are constructed using large quantities of pressed woods and then kept closed up. Kitchens and bathrooms have higher temperatures and humidity than other rooms in the house, resulting in an increase in the rate of formaldehyde release. The concentration is even greater when the rooms are small with minimal ventilation. The new baby's bedroom that is freshly painted and has new particleboard shelves, with both the paint and the particleboard releasing formaldehyde, is another concern. Our research has indicated that the highest levels of formaldehyde are found in bedrooms, probably because of the built-in wardrobes and other furniture and the fact that bedroom doors are often kept closed.

Effects of formaldehyde

Of even greater concern is the level of formaldehyde in new caravans and transportable buildings. The high percentage of new particleboard and plywood used in their construction and the very airtight design leads to high concentrations of this toxic chemical. The research we have conducted has found levels that regularly exceed the indoor air guidelines even with the doors and windows open. In one case, a camper van was freshly renovated with a new particleboard and plywood interior. The driver became sick every time he went on holidays, suffering headaches, eye, nose and throat irritation and nausea. Upon removal of the pressed wood, symptoms ceased and never reoccurred.

In a new office building we were asked to investigate why people on the fourth floor were feeling sick. All the occupants on that floor had symptoms ranging from mild irritation to headache and nausea. The cause was the new office furniture, which was emitting formaldehyde from both the wood and the fresh polish and lacquer. One year later many people still suffered: some had increased sensitivities to a wide range of chemicals.

While the US and Europe have national standards for formaldehyde release from pressed wood products, Australia and New Zealand have only voluntary industry guidelines. These guidelines are substantially lower than the overseas standards, allowing higher levels of emissions. This is further compounded by the increasing amount of pressed wood being imported from Asia where there are even fewer controls in place.

Chapter 7. Volatile Organic Compounds (VOCs)

Volatile organic compounds are a class of carbon-based chemicals, which evaporate easily at room temperature, giving off vapours that can be inhaled. Houses, offices, trains and car interiors all contain substances that emit VOCs. This is the penalty we pay for the "convenience" of our lifestyles, yet it is becoming obvious that the burden of serious illness is a heavy one indeed.

VOC cocktails

There are many sources of VOCs and with so many of these sources present in our homes and offices, various cocktails of these compounds are formed. It is often very difficult to identify the source of a particular compound and at present we have no way of measuring how dangerous these cocktails are to human health. Testing for the various health effects of VOCs is very expensive and difficult.

New buildings especially emit large amounts of VOCs. Building materials such as plywood boards and polystyrene insulation boards are major sources, with VOC off-gassing from the sealants of wooden and parquetry floors, paints, lacquers, varnishes and adhesives. The indoor air quality is made even more toxic by having the windows closed during any coating process. Cleaning products (floor cleaners, waxes, deodorisers, carpet cleaners, furniture polish) emit large amounts of VOCs. Consumer products such as polyvinyl floor coverings and polyvinyl coated wallpapers and the building products already mentioned emit compounds such as xylene, toluene, ethyl benzene, styrene and methyl acetate. Carpets are another major source of VOCs, although the true source is often the glues or underlay.

Table I. Common sources of VOCs

Non-stick cooking aerosols	Degreasers	Aerosol pain relievers
Aerosol antiperspirant	Wax strippers	Aerosol fly sprays
Shoe polish	Liquid waxes	Dry-cleaning fluids
Refrigerants	Hair sprays	Aerosol paints
Sanitizers	Paint lacquers	Anti-cough aerosols
Typewriter correction fluid	Lighter fluids	Room deodorizers
Felt tip pens	Polishes	Contact cements
Aerosol deodorants	Disinfectants	Photocopy machines
Nail polish remover	Gasoline	Printers
New furniture	New appliances	New computers
Smoking	Cleaning products	Cooking methods

Toxic effects

Chemicals are used in the production of nearly all (except for the truly "green") 21st century products because of their seemingly useful properties. For example, solvents are used because they easily dissolve other chemicals. Unfortunately, it is these properties that contribute to adverse health effects.

Typical health properties of VOCs include:

- Lipophilic: with the ability to pass through lipid layers these have an affinity for nerve tissue;
- Soluble in blood and able to pass rapidly through lung tissue; and
- Unobjectionable odour: they are unlikely to provoke irritation or even be noticed until high concentrations are reached.

These properties give VOCs the potential of causing widespread damage to the human body. During exposure the chemical is often not noticed—and in some cases it is even preferred, for example in the case of the "new car smell." The chemical is rapidly absorbed through the skin if in liquid form or through the lungs if in vapour form. It will easily pass into the blood and circulate through the body, passing through the blood-brain barrier. Finally, prolonged exposure may induce an addictive effect in the exposed individual and damage to the nervous system.

VOCs have typically been associated with Sick Building Syndrome in new and refurbished buildings. They can irritate the mucous membranes of the eyes, nose and throat causing headaches and respiratory distress and they can impair thinking and concentration, resulting in mental fatigue and confusion. Because many VOCs are respiratory irritants they trigger an inflammatory response in the upper air passages. Most of the volatile organic compounds identified in indoor air can be respiratory irritants under certain conditions and in certain concentrations. In new and renovated office buildings, the most frequent complaints are mucous membrane irritation and dryness of the eyes and nose.

Because exposure to VOCs may induce an inflammatory response in the airways, there is an increased health risk for people with particular respiratory problems living in newer homes. Our research identified increased lower airway inflammation in non-asthmatic children in new homes. Other research has shown that individuals with pre-existing conditions, such as asthma, may be at increased risk when there is chronic, low-level exposure to the irritating gases of volatile organic compounds.

But these are not the only dangers of VOCs. Various low-level neurotoxic effects have also been reported. These include headaches, sleepiness, tremors and twitches, inability to concentrate, poor memory and irritability. VOCs can cause irritation of membranes and tissues by extracting the fat, or lipid, portion from the membrane. This defatting of the skin causes cell damage and can cause serious injuries to the skin, lungs and eyes.

The "sink effect"

To complicate matters further, certain objects and materials are able to both emit VOCs and absorb them from the air (this is called the "sink effect"). Absorbed VOCs off-gas again later. These sink and multi-layering effects are the subjects of a great deal of research at the present time, as they are not fully understood.

A major problem in understanding and measuring complex mixtures of indoor pollutants is that some people will be affected while others will have no symptoms at all. While we are able to understand some of the effects of acute exposure to individual VOCs, little is known about acute or chronic exposure to hundreds of volatile organic compounds at low concentrations. With elevated levels of prolonged exposure to these chemicals, it is not surprising that National Science reports that approximately 15 percent of the population has an increased sensitivity to low-dose pollutants.

Sources of Volatile Organic Compounds (VOCs)

Water

A major source of exposure to VOCs is water. Chlorine is added to water to prevent serious waterborne diseases rife in many developing countries. However, it also reacts with the organic materials in the water to produce a range of organochlorine chemicals. These include chloroform and a group of chemicals called trihalomethanes including trichloroethane and trichloro-ethylene.

Concern about the chemicals in our water has caused many people to install filters for drinking water. Of equal importance, however, is exposure to these chemicals during showering. These compounds evaporate readily out of warm water. In addition, when warm, pressurised water makes contact with the walls and floor of the shower, then microscopic aerosols form, containing more chemicals and gases. In a shower of three minutes a person might breathe 150 litres of contaminated air.

Chloroform is a suspected carcinogen that is likely to cause cancer. At high concentrations it is an irritant and central nervous system and cardiac depressant. Conjunctivitis may occur from exposure to its vapours. Chronic exposure in low concentrations can lead to both liver and kidney toxicity. Tri-chloroethylene is a potent liver carcinogen and attacks the central and peripheral nervous systems. At high concentrations it can cause dizziness, headache, vertigo, light central nervous system depression and even loss of consciousness.

Reducing your exposure to these organochlorines requires removal of chlorine using a filter if possible or at least ensuring good ventilation when you shower. Install an extractor fan if you don't already have one in the bathroom. Have the fan operating and, to improve ventilation further, open a window.

Plastics

Phthalates are esters of phthalic acid and are used to give plastic compounds their flexibility or softness. The largest single use of phthalates is in the manufacture of polyvinyl chlorides (PVCs) used in wires and cables, floor tiles, upholstery, hoses, food wraps and containers. Dioctyl phthalate (DOP) represents approximately 25 percent of all phthalates consumed and is used in the products mentioned above, as well as in paints, sporting goods and personal care and children's products. Manufacturers use DEHP—in quantities as high as 50 percent of product contents—to achieve a desired degree of plasticity for specific products.

The toxic effect of phthalates on plants has been known since 1949. However, incidents of contamination are still being reported. Contamination of greenhouse plastics, pot containers and PVC pipe used for irrigating plants has resulted in severe adverse effects often leading to death of the plants. The toxic effect on humans is not well understood. Phthalates and other VOCs are emitted from computers as well as from other plastic surfaces as they heat up. Generally, the older the plastic is, the lower the emissions.

Offices

The exhaust from wet process copying machines is a major source of volatile organic compounds in office buildings. Compounds such as benzene, toluene, 2,2,4-trimethyl heptane and isodiene vapours are emitted from the machines' processes.

Effects of these gases include respiratory system, eye, nose and throat irritation along with adverse effects on the nervous system. These problems are likely to occur when people are located close to photocopiers in a small room with inadequate ventilation.

Cars

Motor vehicles are another source of VOCs in houses and office blocks, especially those with sealed garages or car parks where the exhaust fumes are trapped. The plastics in new cars are also a significant source of exposure. In our research we have identified symptoms including nausea, irritability and difficulty in concentrating in people exposed to new car smells. In one case a family had two new cars but could not use either one because both adults in the family were sensitive to the off-gassing from the plastics and vinyls in the new vehicles.

Carpets

Carpets are a major source of volatile organic compounds because of the products used in their manufacture, the large surface area that they cover in many homes and, in particular, the adhesives and solvents used in having them installed. High concentrations of chemicals are often connected with the strong odours typical of new carpets. Many carpets have reclaimed rubber or foam latex backing made of recycled rubber, or synthetic rubber with fillers and additives. Almost all tufted and non-woven carpets have a coating of latex or PVCs added to the primary backing to strengthen the tuft anchorage. Woven carpets are often coated on the back with starch solutions, sometimes combined with latex or resin. Carpets can contain chemicals such as benzene, styrene, xylene, n-decane, n-undecane, dichloroethane and tetrachloroethylene.

Carpets are a notorious cause of Sick Building Syndrome. Many carpet problems are linked to 4-phenylcyclohexene (4-PC). Levels of 4-PC as low as 17 parts per trillion may cause eye and respiratory irritation and levels as low as five parts per trillion may cause reactions in sensitive individuals. The major emissions come from carpet adhesives, especially from the solvent used in carpet backing, as well as the glues used in fixing them to the floor.

Paints

Paints are essentially a liquid plastic coating derived from petroleum. Even when the paint has apparently dried it continues to off-gass volatile chemicals into the air. Off-gassing of paints may last days or, under some conditions, even months, meaning that the occupants of the building are chronically exposed. Even the so-called "water based" paints are nothing more than plastic resins (such as acrylic) dissolved with low odour solvents (such as glycol ethers) to make them "water thinnable."

The synthetic paint industry has over 1,000 substances to choose from to make its products. Some of the dangerous ingredients found in synthetic paints and varnishes are cadmium, styrene, benzene, formaldehyde, toluene, xylene, ethylene glycol, isocyanates (the chemicals responsible for the world's worst industrial accident, Bhopal), chromates, mineral turpentine and pentachlorophenol.

Toxic effect

The Painters' Hazards Handbook put out by the Operative Painters and Decorators Union lists five main health hazards associated with the ingredients in synthetic paints. These are occupational cancer, "Painters' Syndrome" (brain and central nervous system damage), skin diseases, lung diseases and reproductive hazards.

Consumers exposed to paints, lacquers and varnishes have reported headaches, memory troubles, nausea and long-term health problems. A recent study also found increased respiratory problems in children residing in freshly painted homes. Some years ago my colleagues and I investigated a retail paint store where the manager complained of frequent headaches, concentration and memory problems and tremors. His tremors were worse later in the day and toward the end of the week. All the symptoms disappeared whenever he was absent from work. Even if he had a busy work schedule he was symptom-free when he was away from the shop. His symptoms were caused by continual exposure to the VOCs emitted from paints.

As mentioned in the section on formaldehyde, a common problem we have come across is when expecting parents paint the baby's room. Not only is it toxic to the newly born baby but also to the pregnant mother and the developing foetus. Many of these chemicals cross the placenta into the unborn child.

Alternatives

Alternatives to these petroleum products include plant-based paints, made from a selection of approximately 150 raw materials of plant and mineral origin. While it is not intended to suggest in any way that plant-based products are totally safe, it is interesting to note that a great number of the ingredients are either used as food or authorised for use as food additives. For example, linseed oil (the oldest known food oil), soya bean lecithin, casein (made from cow's milk), beeswax, orange peel oil, shellac, carnauba wax, chalk, lemon oil, bergamot oil and iron oxides are among the ingredients. It is also interesting to note that one brand of paints, Livos Plant Chemistry, is deemed so safe it is exempt from Material Safety Data sheets in all countries where it is sold. Indeed, increased awareness about the dangers of chemical-based paint has led to a few of the bigger commercial paint companies now producing safer, low-VOC paints.

Cosmetics

Today, millions of consumers use cosmetics and other personal care products. Toiletries like hair sprays, perfumes and deodorants are designed with pleasant, fresh smells, which are supposed to make us feel good. It is ironic that they are actually emitting chemicals that can cause health problems. Many of these chemicals are quickly taken into the lungs and absorbed into the blood.

Many cosmetics contain dangerous chemicals. Formaldehyde is used primarily as a preservative in thousands of cosmetics including shampoo, mascara, creams (especially anti-aging creams) and nail products. Acetone, typically used in nail polish remover, readily forms a gas and can cause adverse effects on the nervous system. PVP (polyvinyl pyrrolidine) is a suspected human teratogen and carcinogen and is found mostly in hair sprays and also in foundations, shampoos and face creams.

Occupational hazards

A significant and growing percentage of the population reacts to these chemicals. Typical symptoms of exposure include irritation of the eyes, nose and throat, allergic type responses and respiratory problems. Beauticians and hairdressers, who constantly work with cosmetic products, are faced with the cumulative effects of exposure to these toxic substances. Long-term studies of female beauticians have shown a high risk of cancer in the uterus and ovaries as well as breast, digestive and respiratory cancer, including lung cancer.

Chapter 8. Cleaning Products

The reason we use so many toxic cleaning chemicals in our homes is that we have been sold fear by the industries selling the products. They try to make us feel inadequate, dirty and paranoid about a few smells or bacteria in the home when the greatest health risk comes from the chemicals they sell. This is not to say that we can ignore home hygiene, rather, we just don't need these chemicals. It is all media hype.

Cleaning products are one of the most hazardous yet widely used commodities in our homes and "cleaning" with them will cause indoor pollution as well as environmental pollution. In the United States the Consumer Product Safety Commission, working under guidelines of the Federal Hazardous Substance Act, regulates cleaning products. In Australia there is no government body that regulates the chemicals going into cleaning products; all that is prescribed is an incomplete list of the chemicals that should not be used! This gives manufacturers great freedom to determine which chemicals to put in their products - including new chemicals and untested combinations of chemicals - leaving you, the consumer, guessing what is actually in the bottles and packets you buy. There are approximately 250 chemicals in per household which, if ingested, could send a person to hospital or possibly kill a small child. For example, in the United States a child swallows a poisonous substance every 60 seconds and accidental household poisonings are the fourth highest cause of death in England and Wales after traffic accidents, falls and suicides. Approximately 7,000 people in Australia attend accident and emergency departments at hospitals each year as a result of accidental poisoning by household chemicals. Few people realise that swallowing cleaning products can be fatal. In the meantime, intentional use of cleaning products to achieve a dangerous "high" is on the rise in the United States and elsewhere.

Toxic effects

Direct contact with cleaning products is known to cause allergic or irritant dermatitis. When we use them we also inhale the gases they emit. Cleaning products are invariably perfumed. Perfumes that may cause an allergic reaction include balsam of Peru, wood tars and benzyl salicylate. Some perfumes in cleaning products contain phenyl acetaldehyde, a proven sensitiser, and one of the dozens of potentially toxic chemicals used in combination to manufacture any one fragrance. The effect of chemical cocktails like these on human health is untested. In an experiment in the US, cleaning agents and insecticides used within the indoor environment emitted high concentrations of chemicals. High levels of chloroform1, 2-dichlorethane, trichloroethane and carbon tetrachloride were observed.

Solvents are among the most toxic ingredients found in cleaning products. Exposure at high enough levels can lead to a range of effects including euphoria, giddiness, headaches, nausea and even unconsciousness. They can act as depressors on the central nervous system. Acute exposure may lead to haemorrhaging.

Disinfectants usually contain volatile chemicals with the most common being cresol, phenol, ethanol, formaldehyde, ammonia and chlorine. Toxic effects include damage to the liver, kidneys, lungs, pancreas and spleen. They also affect the central nervous system, resulting in depression and irritability.

In a study carried out in a hospital where a borax (mineral) solution was used as a disinfectant the results showed the same biological standard as the manufactured chemical disinfectants, without the added risk of increasing a person's chemical sensitivity while vulnerable and infirm. A series of tests on disinfectants in the US showed the majority were ineffective. Sometimes it is a good idea to use the products that grandma used - mostly lots of water.

All-purpose cleaners often contain chemicals such as ammonia, petroleum distillates, phenol, kerosene, pentachlorophenol and formaldehyde. Toxic effects include rashes, chemical burns and irritation of the eyes and lungs. If cleaners contain petroleum distillates they can cause fatal lung conditions.

Carpet floor cleaners may include formaldehyde, perchloroethylene (a known human carcinogen), ethanol, ammonia and detergents. Immediate effects through direct contact and inhalation include light-headedness, dizziness, appetite loss, disorientation and potential long-term damage to the liver or central nervous system.

Floor wax is a combination of 1, 4 diethyl benzene, butyl benzene, decane, 1, 2, 5 trimethylbenzene, 1-nonene, ethyl benzene, xylene and limonene. Inhalation of ethyl benzene has produced fatigue, insomnia, headaches and mild irritation of the eyes and the respiratory tract. At high levels, ethyl benzene can cause membrane irritation, central nervous system depression, and pathological changes in the liver and kidney.

Air fresheners are perhaps the most insidious of the indoor air pollutants. This is because the chemicals are purposefully released into a confined indoor environment (including many vehicles). Their release under pressure (spraying) creates microscopic particles that can fill a room in seconds. These small aerosolised particles are readily inhaled deep into the lungs and enter the bloodstream. Air fresheners may include formaldehyde, ethanol, phenol, naphthalene, cresol and xylene. Toxic effects include nerve deadening, which affects ability to smell by coating the nasal passages with an undetectable oil film. Aerosols themselves can result in heart problems as well as in problems in virtually all of the body's other organs.

Chapter 9. Detergents

Detergents in all forms—liquids, cakes or powders—are mistakenly accepted as safe and convenient household products (even though many have environmental problems related to their biodegradability and phosphate content), often because they are sold at the local supermarket.

Household toxicity has generally been connected with accidental swallowing or minor irritations such as dermatitis. However, extensive research including our own is now showing a direct link with the number of cleaning chemicals and the risk of allergies, asthma and other adverse health effects. Some preliminary research is also showing a link with cancers. Further, in the cleaning products industry, it is widely accepted that detergent manufacture poses risks in the form of respiratory and skin sensitisation.

An examination of the ingredients in detergents and new research regarding secondary effects of using these products reveal that there could be some serious toxicological problems related to detergent use. For instance, liquid detergents release benzene vapours that could pose a carcinogenic risk to users. It also appears that as detergents break down in waterways they release hormone mimics that can interfere with the normal reproductive functions of human beings. Research is only just beginning to address some of these problems. In many areas there is still a grave paucity of knowledge, meaning that many people may unknowingly be putting themselves at risk.

Toxic ingredients in laundry and dishwashing detergents include:

- Bleaching agents

- Fluorescents

- Zeolites (Sodium Aluminosilicate)—although largely removed in sewage treatment, their effect on the environment remains unknown

- Perfumes and colorants

- Petrochemicals

- Solvents such as benzene

- Polymers

- Enzymes

- Hormone mimics

- Phenol

- Toluene

- Xenoestrogens

As detergents break down in waterways they release seemingly innocuous substances, which in turn break down into nonylphenol, an oestrogen-like substance. These types of chemicals have been named synthetic or foreign oestrogens, xenoestrogens or endocrine disrupters. Because they are so similar in structure to the oestrogen produced by our bodies, our cells will receive xenoestrogens and try to make use of them. Although similar to oestrogen in structure, they are synthetic compounds and have many unwanted and unpleasant side effects. Once introduced into our bodies they can alter our hormonal activity, disrupting our normal reproductive functioning.

Dishwashing detergents emit vapours of xylene, n-undecane and n-dodecane. Laboratory tests on rats and mice have shown immune system suppression and the possible development of cancers after exposure to such detergents. Dishwashing detergents are particularly insidious because the user is in close contact with the products and usually inhaling the chemicals in them from the steam rising from the hot water in the sink. This problem is exacerbated by the fact that pleasant, "natural" scents are (chemically) added to mask any chemical smells and to give the perception of improved cleaning.

Most laundry detergents are produced entirely from petrochemicals or coal and contain a large number of ingredients, a high percentage of which are either toxins or have an indirect detrimental effect on the environment. An average laundry detergent composition includes 15% to 25% synthetic surfactant, 30% to 40% condensed phosphate, 5% anti-corrosive silicate and 1% or less of anti-redeposition and optical brightener.

Within these basic categories is an impressive list of toxic chemicals including xylene, n-undecane, n-dodecane and benzene vapours which can cause increase in weight (YES, weight gain!), decrease in white blood cells (shown in rats) and the promotion of tumour activity in mice. Phenol, sodium nitrate, ethanol, sulphuric acid and caustic soda are also common ingredients and are either toxic or combine to create toxic compounds.

Detergent residues in clothes and linen can cause skin irritation such as rashes, itchiness and inflammation. I have often been asked to resolve skin rash problems so the first thing I do is encourage an individual to use fewer and safer detergents. This, in many cases, is a simple strategy that works.

In Japan there have been tests on pregnant mice where exposure to everyday laundry detergents resulted in 100 percent of the embryos haemorrhaging, 70 percent having spinal deformities and 40 percent having harelips and other deformities. Two percent had brains protruding through or completely outside the skull. A high proportion of the mature mice suffered disorders of the internal organs. Male mice had reduced sperm production, shortened tails, malformed heads and altered DNA structures. Another study showed workers with four to 27 years of exposure to the manufacture of soaps and detergents had a higher than normal rate of laryngeal cancer and lung cancer.

Abuse of laundry products can often lead to hospitalisation. Detergents are poisonous if swallowed and children are particularly susceptible. Swallowing liquid detergents commonly leads to nausea, vomiting and diarrhoea. Powder detergents are far more dangerous as they can burn the mouth and throat.

Laundry detergents contain some products that have a history of being toxic to humans plus other substances, the use of which has been restricted (i.e., phenol is contained in some detergents but its use in cosmetic products that come in contact with the skin has been restricted in the UK).

Getting in

There are basically three paths by which any toxin is taken up by a living organism: by swallowing or otherwise injecting the toxin, by absorbing it across the skin or by inhaling the vapours. Detergents would not normally be swallowed unless by accident. However, traces of detergents and their components are now found in most drinking water due to normal disposal processes. There is also the possibility of detergents and their components entering waterways in greater concentrations through accidental leaks and spillages at manufacturing sites. This has happened in relation to many detergent components. Phenol, for instance, has been involved in at least three separate industrial spillages in the US, and widespread poisoning was reported after local populations ingested the substance through the water supply.

In the case of direct accidental swallowing, detergents can be highly corrosive. Bleaches contained in laundry powders contain strong oxidising agents such as sodium perborate. Bleach is an irritant and will cause vomiting if accidentally swallowed. If detergents are swallowed there is the possibility of surfactants entering the circulatory system. Here they can cause damage— including cell destruction—in even very low concentrations.

Once ingested, whether by accidental swallowing or through the trace amounts found in drinking water, the toxins in detergents vary in their rate of absorption in the human body. The solvents, including benzene and xylene, contained in detergents are highly volatile, making them easily absorbed after ingestion. Of concern is absorption of benzene due to its carcinogenic nature and xylene because it is suspected to cause birth defects.

Direct contact with detergents is known to cause allergic reactions. In fact, 15 to 30 percent of people in developed countries suffer allergies and related diseases and many people are now questioning the extent to which household chemicals are responsible. While detergents would certainly not be the cause of all these reactions, relationships have been shown between detergents containing caustic alkaline substances and allergic or irritant dermatitis.

Under certain conditions, excessive exposure to soap and detergents leads to changes in the skin. The severity of the reaction will be influenced by environmental conditions, physical health (e.g., stress) and contact with other cleaning agents such as bleaches and abrasives. Surfactants in detergents appear to be one factor in skin irritation. They have been shown to reduce the lipid barrier of the skin after prolonged contact leading to loss of moisture, increased permeability of the skin, dryness, and roughness and flaking.

This means that a significant proportion of the population is being put at risk through the breakdown of this important barrier. The skin prevents or slows down the entry of many toxins into the body. Damage to the skin's horny protective layer through detergent-related dermatitis is a serious condition because it gives chemicals easy access to the living cells below. People so affected by dermatitis should be particularly careful in handling chemicals due to increased vulnerability.

It is not only direct contact with detergents but inhalation of vapours from liquid detergents and dusts from powders that can cause problems. Vapours from detergents can persist in the air for several hours.

Ammonia is found in oven cleaners, multipurpose cleaners and cloudy ammonia. Toxic effects include eye and nose irritation if contact is made with the vapour. Effects depend on level of exposure; for example, one percent in the air causes mild irritation and three percent in the air produces stinging sensations. Exposure to ammonia can cause headaches and vomiting and, in high concentrations, lung damage.

Solvents are highly volatile which makes them easily absorbed through the lungs. For example, 50 percent of toluene would be retained if inhaled. Benzene fumes in liquid detergents are easily inhaled by humans. In fact, benzene can be found in the exhaled air of a person using a product containing benzene. The danger with detergents is that it appears a higher proportion of benzene is converted to toxic metabolites at low doses than at high doses. Xylenes are readily absorbed through inhalation but it appears high doses are needed before chronic effects on the central nervous system and mucous membranes are observed. Xylene fumes are irritants of the eyes, nose and lungs.

Sodium nitrilotriacetate (NTA), present as a builder in laundry detergents, has been linked to tumour formation in animal studies. NTA is not fully removed in wastewater treatment and, as a result, NTA is now present in drinking supplies of countries that recycle water.

There is also danger in some of the perfumes used in detergents, such as nitro musks. Nitro musks are not easily biodegradable and can accumulate in breast milk. German studies found high levels in breast milk, which raised concerns about possible health effects. As a result, some manufacturers are now phasing out such perfumes.

Enzymes appear to contribute to asthma and an increase in respiratory disorders. The effect of enzymes appears irreversible in humans. While the risk increases with concentrations inhaled, symptoms can disappear after exposure, only to reappear again after re-exposure at low levels. Enzymes have been further connected with the incidence of asthma in detergent industry workers. While respiratory problems originally appeared to be reversible after removal from exposure, studies have found long-term respiratory loss in some individuals. As a result the use of enzymes in the detergent industry has been the subject of bans since 1971. This action led to Australian detergent manufacturers ceasing the manufacture of enzyme-containing detergents. However, importing detergents containing enzymes has continued.

Reproductive effects

Another problem with detergents is that seemingly innocuous ingredients can break down under normal usage conditions into nonylphenol, an oestrogen mimic. Nonylphenols are the breakdown products of alkylphenol polyethoxylates (APEOs) a type of surfactant used in washing detergents and dishwashing liquids. These types of chemicals have been named synthetic or foreign estrogens, xenoestrogens or endocrine disruptors. Once introduced into the body they can mimic the action of oestrogen produced normally in cells or alter hormonal activity. They do this by binding with and activating oestrogen receptors.

It appears that only relatively small exposures to these nonylphenols are needed to trigger reproductive effects compared with carcinogenic effects. For example, prenatal exposure to these endocrine disruptors can interfere with the normal establishment of gender and reproductive factors.

Environmental hormones such as nonylphenols appear to be increasing the risk of reproductive system abnormalities. Some reported effects include testicular cancer, undescended testes, urinary tract defects and lowered sperm counts. There is a particularly strong link with breast cancer. When these substances are introduced into the body they mimic the action of oestrogen and alter the hormone's activity.

Their potential link to hormonally induced abnormalities was first questioned when populations of wildlife in contaminated environments showed symptoms of abnormal sexual development. One example that may have been linked to detergent by-products was the production of vitellogenin, a female protein, by male fish living near municipal sewer outlets. While the scientific community is still debating the causes of such disruptions, some of the defects have been reproduced in experiments with animals exposed to nonylphenol. Field and laboratory studies tend to suggest that endocrine-disrupting substances can contribute to breast cancer in women and reproductive abnormalities in men.

One of the major problems with assessing the toxicity of detergents is that few studies have been carried out, especially in the Australian environment. Those studies that do exist have identified a range of toxic effects from detergents including remobilisation of metals, reduced rates of biodegradability and decreased effectiveness of sewage treatment with the potential for more toxins to be released into the environment. Detergents appear to act in synergy with other chemicals, compounding their toxicity. They have been shown to be toxic to aquatic invertebrates, fish and plants.

However, great variation in the toxicity of detergents has been found, which may be explainable by their individual chemical compositions. The ingredients that cause detergents to be so toxic still raise questions. According to one study, substances previously believed to affect the toxicity of detergents such as plaorus, enzymes and zeolites did not appear to be the major toxins. Variation in toxicity may be due to other factors such as surfactants. While surfactants are generally well tolerated at the concentration levels found in detergents, the structure of some of these compounds appears to make them toxic.

Clearly, much broader research is needed on the general toxicity of detergents. Despite this, current study of some of the active ingredients in detergents has helped form a picture of the potential toxicity of detergent products.

Regulations

Most of the regulations relating to detergents address its manufacture and disposal, rather than household usage. Areas with a great deal of controversy in relation to standards include biodegradability, phosphate contents, the use of enzymes and regulation of carcinogenic ingredients.

In response to environmental concerns, Australian detergent manufacturers have introduced a phosphorous labelling scheme. "NP" indicates no phosphorus or up to 0.5%. "P" indicates a level up to 5%. The labelling system appears to have been effective in encouraging detergent manufacturers to reduce phosphate content in their products.

Another area where attempts to set standards have been made is in relation to enzymes. The Australian recommended concentration in laundry detergents of 0.05% by weight. However as no legal limit has been set, manufacturers could increase the level of enzymes, particularly as demand for concentrated products increases.

Chapter 10. Pesticides

Pesticides are a major concern because we are using more every year. Many people incorrectly think that, because these chemicals are available in the hardware shops or even from chemists, they are safe. They are not. They are toxic products designed to kill insects. What the pesticide industry does not want you to know is that, in fact, insects and humans have a lot in common. This is especially apparent with the nervous system. Many insecticides that are designed to attach to the nervous system of flies and cockroaches also damage our nervous systems. The situation becomes worse when we use them in our homes because they stay in the air and we spend so much time at home so we, along with our kids, are continually inhaling these poisons. There are much safer techniques available (e.g., sticky traps for cockroaches and ants).

Recent research suggests that up to 80 percent of most people's exposure to airborne pesticides occur indoors. Research in Australia in the mid-1980s identified that the organochlorine pesticides used for termite control were found in high levels in homes and consequently at high levels in the milk of breast-feeding mothers. Our research also found that these chemicals could still be detected even 10 years after use for termite treatment.

While we have moved to less persistent pesticides, the currently used toxic chemicals can stay around for weeks, months and even years. The reason we overuse and abuse these chemicals is that we have often become fearful of insects and pests but paradoxically the pesticide is often more dangerous than the pest!

Toxic effects

Pesticides are toxic. They are designed to kill and with biology and biochemistry they affect humans the same way they affect insects. A pesticide is any substance or mixture of substances intended for preventing, destroying, repelling or mitigating pests.

Pesticides cover several broad chemical categories. The major groups are the inorganic and organic chemicals. The inorganic category (containing no carbon) includes substances that have been used as insecticides and fungicides since ancient times. Generally they include minerals and heavy metals such as copper, zinc, boron, sulphur, arsenic, iron, cyanide, lead, mercury and sodium. During the 19th and 20th centuries compounds of these substances were developed as pesticides. These included calcium arsenate, lead arsenate, hydrogen cyanide, lime sulphur, salts and various metals (copper sulphate, iron sulphate), organic mercurials and copper silicate. However, like their predecessors, they were often toxic to mammals and were used in excessive quantities that left persistent residues in the environment.

The 1940s and 1950s saw the demise of these inorganic pesticides as the new breed of "organic" pesticides (not be confused with "organic" as it is used in terms of certifying, for example, organically grown produce) were researched and developed. These include the organochlorine (or chlorinated hydrocarbon), organophosphate, carbamate and synthetic pyrethroid pesticides.

This newer class of pesticides can cause a range of acute health effects (the result of a single heavy exposure) or chronic health effects that result from numerous low exposures over a period of time. Symptoms vary according to the pesticide used, the degree of exposure and the amount that gets into the body. They are often non specific and a number of diseases may produce similar symptoms. The most common classes of pesticides kill by damaging the nervous system and, in humans, can cause headaches, nausea, dizziness and poor coordination. Long term exposure can cause a range of adverse effects on human health, including damage to the nervous system, reproductive dysfunction, immune and endocrine problems and some forms of cancer.

For several decades, the nervous system has been a target organ for pesticide toxicity. The brain and the nervous system are the two primary targets of pesticides. Depending on the individual and the type of exposure, typical symptoms include poor memory; inability to concentrate; paraesthesia (nerve tingling and numbness); anxiety; depression; hyperacusis (noises seem louder than they are); fatigue and ataxia (poor balance).

In addition to the neurologic signs and symptoms of acute intoxication, studies have shown that many of the pesticides directed at the nervous system may cause delayed polyneuropathy neurobehavioral effects. Other studies have shown a link between chronic exposure to pesticides and the development of Parkinson's disease and motor neuron disease. Parkinson's disease, a nervous system disorder, decreases muscle control and can eventually disable a person.

The ability of pesticides to damage the immune system and to cause hypersensitivity reactions is often overlooked. The age categories most at risk for immune system damage are infants and children under ten. This is true because their immune systems are very immature and at high risk for damage caused by pesticide exposure. Unfortunately, few epidemiological studies focusing on immune system damage have been conducted on human populations. However, wildlife and animal studies provide us with substantial evidence that pesticides are indeed immunotoxic. More epidemiological studies on humans need to be conducted in this area of concern.

Exposure to pesticides can result in sterility, infertility and gene malformations. Over the past fifty years, measures of male fertility have decreased dramatically worldwide. It is hypothesized that synthetic estrogens, also referred to as endocrine disrupters, are the reason behind this dramatic decrease in male sperm counts. Many endocrine disrupters are pesticides such as 2,4 D, atrazine, benomyl, carbaryl, endosulfan, parathion and synthetic pyrethroids. A recent study found that male members of the Danish Organic Farmers' Association had sperm densities double those found in males who did not consume organically grown food.

Other hormonal disturbances can occur as a result of pesticide exposure. It has been demonstrated that synthetic chemicals such as pesticides, which are harmless on their own, may disrupt the female hormone system when they are combined with other chemicals.

A study published the journal Occupational and Environmental Medicine showed that children frequently exposed to insecticides used in the house, garden and in head lice shampoos run double the risk of developing childhood leukaemia. The latest study by France's National Institute for Medical Research showed that the risk of developing acute leukaemia was almost twice as likely in children whose mothers said that they had used insecticides in the home while pregnant and long after their children's birth. With rates of childhood leukaemia rising most health professionals are trying to find new, great discoveries to cure it. We suggest the best strategy is to reduce your child's exposure to toxic chemicals.

Pesticides can pose a significantly greater threat to children than to adults. The reason is that in relation to their small body weight, children inhale or ingest a greater percentage of toxins than adults do. The playing habits of children such as somersaults on carpets, running barefoot on lawns or digging through dirt give more direct contact with pesticide residues. Exposure of children to home-based pesticide residues (i.e., after household items are treated with pest control products) is generally high as compared to adults since children tend to play in areas that have been sprayed. Research has shown that children living in areas where pesticides had been applied most heavily experienced elevated rates of acute respiratory diseases (including pneumonia), skin diseases, ear infections, tuberculosis and dental caries.

Children receive four times greater exposure to pesticides than adults, because of their small body size and the large amount of fresh fruits and vegetables they consume. Hence children are much more susceptible to carcinogenic substances than adults. In early childhood, cells divide rapidly and this rapid division coupled with exposure to cancer-causing pesticides (e.g., organochlorine) increases the likelihood of cell mutations and the subsequent risk of cancer. Exposure to pesticides during preschool years could lead to cancer later in life.

It is found that half of a lifetime cancer risk from exposure to pesticides occurs during the first six years of life. This exposure also dramatically increases the risk of acute disease.

Pest management in schools

Children are exposed daily to pesticides in food, air, water, homes and on playgrounds; the use of pesticides in and around public buildings such as schools and day care centres is an additional source of exposure. Youngsters are exposed to both indoor and outdoor sources of pesticides, all in the name of controlling insects, weeds and other pests on the school grounds.

Some pesticides can persist in the indoor environment for months or years after application. In addition, tracking may persist on carpets, floors and other surfaces. This can present a relatively important exposure route for children through dermal contact, oral ingestion and inhalation in areas where pesticides are used.

Reducing or eliminating the use of conventional pesticides in schools is not only possible but also is being carried out in a growing number of areas.

Pesticides

The organophosphate pesticide now used to control termites and ants, Chlorpyriphos, persists in homes and continues to expose residents for months or, in some cases, even years. Chlorpyriphos affects the nervous system and is linked with a long list of adverse health effects.

Organophosphate pesticides to look out for:

- Diazinon;
- Dichlorvos; and
- Chlorpyriphos.

Pyrethrum is derived from the dried flowers of Chrysanthemum cineraria folium. The term "pyrethrins" refers to the mixed active ingredients present in commercially available pyrethrum extracts whilst the term "pyrethoids" refers to synthetic analogues of pyrethrin of similar structure to pyrethrums, hence their mode of action is the same.

Pyrethrins are acutely toxic to insects with a high degree of specificity that results from their relative rates of metabolism in insects compared with mammals. This fact has seen pyrethrins labelled as one of the safest and most ideal insecticides. The pyrethroids are metabolised very rapidly in mammals and as a result show only a low potential for bioaccumulation. The half-life of pyrethroids in adipose tissue was calculated at around two weeks. Concern has been raised about a link with the pyrethroids and allergies such as asthma. While these are some of the safest pesticides they should still be used sparingly. A major concern I have is the use of automated pesticides misting machines now being introduced into homes. These machines mist a fine spray of pesticide, often a pyrethrin, into the air every 15 minutes or so and make ridiculous claims about this being safer for the family. Every expose to pesticides increases the toxic load, so stay away from these devices.

Naphthalene is a white crystalline solid that is extracted from the petroleum refining process and coal tar distillation. The Environmental Protection Agency (EPA) classifies it as a Hazardous Substance, Hazardous Waste and Priority Toxic Pollutant. Despite its toxicity it is a common product found in many homes. We most commonly come into contact with naphthalene through the use of mothballs. Some health departments have published advertisements in local papers describing the possible dangers of contact and how to use mothballs correctly. Our personal view is that this chemical cannot be used safely and should not be used in homes.

Naphthalene is an irritant and an allergen; systemically it causes a form of anaemia. Inhalation of greater than 10 parts per million (ppm) can cause headaches, nausea, excessive sweating and vomiting. Naphthalene vapours in the atmosphere greater than 15 ppm can cause eye irritation with severe exposure leading to blurring of vision and injury of the cornea.

Poisoning via ingestion, which can occur with children consuming half a gram of mothballs (because of a candy-like appearance) can induce nausea, vomiting, abdominal pain, irritation of the bladder and brown or black colouration of the urine. In rats and rabbits it has produced cataracts from oral exposure. Naphthalene in high doses in mice reduces the amount of pups, while in humans has been reported to cross the placenta and cause neonatal toxicity.

Another toxic chemical commonly found in the home is arsenic. Arsenic has been used as a treatment for pine to prevent mould and termite attack. It is released into the environment from timber and children playing on arsenic-treated pine playgrounds will be exposed to some degree. Arsenic-treated pine is usually idetifiable by the green colour of the logs or planks. Fortunately CCA (copper chrome arsenic) treated timber is now being phased out. Disposal of the logs is, however, a big problem—burning them creates a highly toxic gas and we shouldn't just dump wood impregnated with this toxic chemical.

Arsenic dust is still used as a bait for termites. Infested areas are treated with a very small amount of arsenic trioxide dust. This is usually not a problem if done professionally and injected into the wood, but no white powder should be visible or left on the outside surfaces.

Arsenic compounds were widely used pharmaceutical agents in the early 1900s. In fact back in 1907, one of the earliest chemotherapy drugs was arsenic. It's a pity we haven't progressed much from there, as some of the current treatments are just as toxic and possibly no more effective.

Arsenic blocks some essential enzymes and inhibits the uptake of selenium, an important anticancer mineral. To protect yourself and your family:

*   Do not buy or use CCA-treated timber; and
*   Do not burn CCA-treated pine timber.

Pentachlorophenol (PCP) is the active component within wood and textile preservatives, and in glues and starches. It also has properties that promote its use as an anti-mould and a fungicide. It is toxic to the liver, kidneys and central nervous system. Chronic high exposure may cause chloracne, sweating, headaches, nausea, loss of mental alertness and loss of muscle control.

Flea control and head lice

Treatment of head lice in children is a perennial problem, but one that requires the upmost caution. Lindane was an organochlorine pesticide commonly used and fortunately now phased out. Malathion is an organophosphate pesticide, occasionally recommended by some naive health departments, which attacks the nervous systems of lice and children. A lot of people think it is safe because it's sold by the chemist; it is not safe. This is apparent if you read the label that says things like, "Wear gloves while applying it to your child's head." This is so parents don't get exposed to the toxic chemicals... but it is okay for a kid to have it soaking though his or her scalp? In addition, because of this chemical's overuse during the past 50 years, lice have developed a resistance to it. We have many people at my talks telling me how they have to use this chemical repeated times and it still does not work. Alternatives are available that are effective, much safer and have been scientifically tested. Quit Nits is a brand of low-toxicity lice treatment that eliminates lice, and it is the only low-toxicity product that we know of that has been shown to be 100 percent effective in clinical trials. It has been tested by one of the leading experts on medical entomology (insects). Preventative treatments are also available for reoccurring problems and the ingredients are so safe that they are edible. For more information visit www.wildchildon-line.com.

Flea control is a major issue in homes with pets. Some of the pesticides on flea collars are highly toxic, exposing the pet as well as the family to the pesticide each time they come close to the pet. Organophosphate, carbamates and pyrethrins are commonly used. New, safer versions use chemicals that break the life and breeding cycles of the fleas.

PART THREE

Chapter 11. Combustion Products

The major combustion products to which we are exposed indoors include nitrogen dioxide, carbon monoxide and various particulates. The sources of these chemical gases in homes include unflued gas heaters and cookers, kerosene heaters, tobacco smoke and garages attached to the office or home.

Nitrogen oxide refers to any compound that contains only nitrogen and oxygen. All nitrogen includes both nitric oxide (NO) and nitrogen dioxide (NO_2). Nitric oxide is a colourless gas which is produced when nitrogen and oxygen combine at high temperatures. On contact with air it is oxidized to form nitrogen dioxide.

Nitrogen dioxide, a pungent, brown, acidic gas, is a serious air pollutant responsible for the formation of acid rain. When it combines with water it forms nitric acid. It is the most common of the nitrogen oxides and it is harmful when inhaled. The major sources of nitrogen dioxide in the home are combustion devices such as gas stoves and unvented gas or kerosene space heaters. (Unflued gas appliances may also contribute to high levels of carbon monoxide indoors.) Health effects related to nitrogen dioxide exposure include impaired lung function and increased bronchial reactivity. Elderly people and those with asthma are especially susceptible to these effects.

The effects of various levels of nitrogen dioxide have been studied since the 1960s because of nitrogen dioxide's injurious effects to the respiratory airways and the fact that it aggravates asthma. Clinical studies have shown a decrease in lung function as a short-term effect of nitrogen dioxide exposure. A study conducted in 1970 was the first to report that children who were exposed to nitrogen dioxide levels typically found in homes (75 ppb to 140 ppb) suffered more respiratory problems than children in general. Many studies have since shown that nitrogen dioxide, even at lower levels, affects children's health, with those under the age of seven having more than twice the normal levels of respiratory problems when exposed to 15 ppb or more of nitrogen dioxide.

A study of the prevalence of respiratory symptoms in South Australian pre-school children between four and five years old, from 14,124 families, found that the at-home use of a natural gas stove, compared to an electric stove, increased the likelihood of a pre-school child having asthma. These findings have been supported by other studies around the world.

Nitrogen dioxide has also been shown to increase the reactivity of the bronchial tubes to substances known to cause allergies in mild asthmatics. This suggests that nitrogen dioxide can aggravate asthmatic responses to allergens such as household dust mites. When we consider that the concentrations of dust to which a person is exposed in the home can be at peak levels, we can see that reducing indoor nitrogen dioxide emissions can be an important factor in managing asthma. Gas heaters may also lead to condensation, which, in turn, can lead to increased mould and dust mite concentrations.

Nitrogen dioxide has also been shown to impair the immune response within the lungs themselves. Macrophages are one of the types of immuno-protective cells in the lining of the alveoli of the lungs; they are white blood cells that scavenge foreign intruders, damaged cells and other debris. They help to suppress infections such as those caused by the influenza virus. However, after exposure to nitrogen dioxide, alveolar macrophages are less effective in suppressing the influenza virus. This is supported by the results of studies that have shown that nitrogen dioxide decreases the immune system's defences against both bacterial and viral pulmonary infections in many different animals. Studies on animals have also shown that prolonged exposure to nitrogen dioxide results in permanent changes in the mucous membranes of the lungs. Other changes include incomplete development of the terminal bronchi, shortened cilia and decreased number of cilia in the respiratory system. The toxicity of nitrogen dioxide is generally attributed to its oxidative and free radical properties.

Some early studies on the level of nitrogen dioxide emissions, in Sydney in 1987, estimated that for several hours every night during the winter, up to half a million Sydney residents were exposed to levels of nitrogen dioxide which exceeded the nationally acceptable level. The emissions were mostly generated from unflued gas heaters.

The toxic effects of nitrogen dioxide are more pronounced with short-term high exposure as compared with long-term (more than 24 hours) low exposure. More recently our research found very high, short-term levels of nitrogen dioxide of 650 ppb associated with gas cookers. Longer term, elevated levels were found with unflued gas heaters. People vulnerable to the toxic and irritant effects of nitrogen dioxide should avoid the kitchen when the stove is in use.

The effect that each source of nitrogen dioxide has on indoor levels depends on frequency and length of use, the conditions under which it is being used as well as the size and ventilation characteristics of the room. Heaters and ovens are typically used for longer periods of time than cookers, so their contribution to indoor levels of nitrogen dioxide is usually greater.

Research has shown that when exhaust fans above the stove are turned on they reduce levels of nitrogen dioxide. However, all too often the exhaust fans work poorly. A good exhaust fan should hold up a piece of light tissue paper. Opening the windows in the kitchen when cooking can provide adequate ventilation. Stoves and heaters with auto-ignition are preferable to those with active, gas burning pilots. Passive solar heaters, gas flued or electric heaters should be used instead of the unflued gas variety.

Of great concern is the increasing tendency toward unflued gas heaters. People may save a little money in the beginning but may have to pay a lot more later as a result of adverse respiratory effects.

Government requirements and regulations

Around Australia, convective gas space heaters (unflued) make up a large portion of the new heater market, despite the trend away from their use overseas and the controversy regarding health effects. Regulations are in place to help protect the consumer with low nitrogen dioxide burner design heaters and minimum ventilation standards upon installation. Every state has regulations governing flueless gas space heaters, including the type of heater (only approved heaters can be installed), heat input into the room, the rooms where installation can occur (including installation of bayonet points) and fixed ventilation requirements. However, there are no assurances that these standards are adopted and there is no information to suggest that elevated levels of nitrogen dioxide do not exist, even if the procedures are followed—in fact our research shows the opposite occurs. In addition, the lack of maintenance of flueless heaters, including the accumulation of dust, plus the fact that they are readily moved and, due to their portability and size, they are more easily damaged all contribute to these units becoming more inefficient and emitting more nitrogen dioxide and carbon monoxide.

The decision to allow these heaters to continue to be installed above any health concerns and without any real knowledge of the concentrations of NO_2 to which people are being exposed appears to be an economic and political decision. Some states are currently phasing them out while others are still allowing them.

Undoubtedly nitrogen dioxide from unflued gas appliances plays a major role in poor indoor air quality and resulting health problems. The Australian gas industry is opposed to stringent indoor standards for nitrogen dioxide, arguing that there is not enough evidence of adverse health effects. This is despite the fact that outdoor standards have been established for many years. The gas industry points the finger at other sources of indoor air pollution; however its economic interests in the sale of gas appliances cannot help but bias its arguments.

In the case of kerosene heaters, there are standards for manufacture but no guidelines on their use. Kerosene heaters are often seen as a cheap and convenient option, but are a major source of toxic gases, including VOCs and nitrogen dioxide and should not be used, as they are the dirtiest of heaters.

Carbon monoxide (CO)

Carbon monoxide (CO) is a chemical asphyxiant gas. CO has an affinity to bind with the haemoglobin in red blood cells at a rate 210 times that of oxygen. The respiratory and cardiovascular systems work together to transport oxygen from ambient air to the various tissues of the body to maintain tissue metabolism. Transport to the tissues can be seriously impaired even at low levels of carbon monoxide exposure. The tissues most sensitive to the effects of CO are the heart and brain.

Acute CO poisoning is responsible for deficits in: visual memory, nonverbal abstraction, planning, attention and concentration, as well as irritability, distractibility, apraxia (lack of coordination of motor functions) and behavioural abnormalities including silly smiles, frowns, repetitive behaviours and loss of social skills. Such effects may also have psychological consequences. Recent research has also shown that acute exposure to CO may lead to Parkinson's disease.

Major sources of CO are outdoor air, kerosene heaters, gas stoves, gas heaters, tobacco smoke, vehicle exhaust and wood stoves. The motor vehicle is the main source of outdoor CO emissions, contributing over 80 percent of CO to the ambient air. Attached garages are a major source of CO in homes. Attached garages with a door leading directly into a house can lead to a slow build-up of toxic CO. If you have an attached garage, do not leave the connecting door open. Warm up your car outside the garage with the exhaust pointing away from the house. While this sounds logical, we see people unwittingly poisoning indoor air with their cars' exhaust fumes every day.

In cars

CO levels inside vehicles are related to outdoor pollution levels. Travel by automobile results in CO exposures approximately twice those of rail commuting and can reach toxic levels quickly in traffic jams. Research we conducted found highest levels when the outside ventilation was on, lower levels when the window was open and lowest levels with recycled air and windows closed. This makes the air stuffy and humid but not toxic. Concentrations typically found in traffic jams may lead to the effects of low-level poisoning such as headache and irritability. Getting stuck in a traffic snarl thus provides several good reasons for being irritable.

Directly linked to the air pollution inside a car are faulty exhaust pipes. If you can smell fumes from your own car, get the exhaust fixed because you are poisoning yourself and your family.

High-rise buildings in cities cause a canyon effect and trap CO, resulting in higher concentrations at street level and the infiltration of CO into buildings on the street. As expected, the highest levels of CO in the streets occur during peak traffic hours. However, the levels in buildings, even in high-rise office buildings, do not peak until one hour or so later. A major source of CO inside buildings is from underground parking areas and garages attached to a main building. Modern underground garages have exhaust fans that are activated when the CO levels reach 50 ppm.

Wood burning heaters

Wood heating has been reported to increase the incidence of chest illnesses in young children. There is a greater incidence of bronchitis, upper respiratory infection and pneumonia amongst the children living in homes where wood is used as a heat source. Researchers also found a higher proportion of chest illness lasting at least one week and a greater proportion of hospitalisations from chest illnesses before the age of two years, compared with children from homes not using wood burning stoves. In one house with an open fire the level of particulates increased to 10 to 30 times the background levels once the open fire was lit. These levels are extremely high and are a major health concern.

Chapter 12. Environmental Tobacco Smoke

The first scientific report linking cancer to tobacco use was issued more than two hundred years ago. Research since then has correlated a number of other diseases and health problems with cigarette smoking. In the past 30 years the industrialised world has witnessed a change in attitude and a trend toward non-smoking. In some less industrialised countries, however, this trend appears to be the reverse.

Please, if you smoke, read this chapter with an open mind and think about how much better your life could be without tobacco! If someone you live with or someone you love smokes find a way to gently, non-judgmentally, share this material with him or her.

Exposure to cigarette smoke occurs in two forms: mainstream and side stream smoke. Mainstream (MS) is the smoke inhaled through the cigarette by the smoker. Side stream smoke (SS) is that released into the external environment by the cigarette and by the smoker. The amount of SS smoke is usually twice the amount of MS. As the SS smoke enters the environment unfiltered, it contains a large concentration of harmful chemicals. The term "passive smoking" refers to the inhalation by non-smokers of SS smoke.

Estimates suggest that there are more than 4,000 components of cigarette smoke with at least 43 known cancer-causing chemicals. The concentrations of these components in MS and SS smoke differ according to the temperature of combustion, degree of filtration and the amount and type of tobacco smoked.

Some of the toxic particles, chemicals and gases found in tobacco smoke include:

Nicotine	N-Nitrosonornicotine
Formaldehyde	Phenol
Carbazole	Benzene
Catechol	N-Methylcarbazole
N-Nitrosodimethylamine	Naphthalene
Indole	N-Nitrosopyrrolidine
Benzo(a)pyrene	N-Methylindole
Acrolein	Aniline
Benz(a)anthracene	Acetone
2-Naphthylamine	Fluorene
Pyridine	4-Aminobiphenyl
Fluoranthene	3-vinyl pyridine
N-Nitrosonornicotine	Chrysene
Isoprene	Cadmium
DDD	Acetaldehyde
Nickel	DDT
Toluene	Zinc
4,4'-Dichlorostilbene	N-Nitrosomethylethylamine
Cholesterol	Carbon monoxide
Hydrazine	o-Cresol
Carbon dioxide	Nitromethane
m- and p-Cresol	Nitrogen oxides
Nitro ethane	2,4-Dimethylphenol
Ammonia	Nitrobenzene
p-Ethylphenol	Hydrogen cyanide

Carbon monoxide (CO)

Carbon monoxide is a colourless, odourless toxic gas. It is a small molecule and is therefore able to pass through a cigarette's filter tip. It is absorbed through the smoke as it is inhaled. CO combines with haemoglobin to form carboxyhaemoglobin and blocks the ability to carry oxygen in the blood. As mentioned above, CO is 210 times more potent in sticking to the haemoglobin than oxygen, which is why people suffocate from CO exposure in circumstances like house fires. People who smoke have been found to have between five and 20 percent concentrations of carboxyhaemoglobin in their blood. This plays a large part in the fatigue felt by smokers.

Nicotine

Nicotine is the addictive component of the cigarette. Initially, it is absorbed by the lungs and enters the bloodstream, then is distributed throughout the body. When nicotine reaches the brain, it attaches to receptors in brain tissue, affecting metabolic and electrical processes in the brain as well as in the nervous system.

The immediate effects include an increased heart rate and blood pressure as the demand by the heart for oxygen increases and epinephrine is released. There is also evidence that blood vessels constrict, reducing the blood supply to the extremities and decreasing the skin temperature. The stimulation of the nervous system by nicotine causes the release of dopamine and noradrenaline. Both of these are linked with a stimulatory effect and with addiction.

The long-term effects of nicotine intake include lung and mouth cancer, respiratory disease, emphysema, bronchitis, heart attacks and poor blood circulation. Aortic ruptures and cerebral aneurisms can occur. Nicotine increases the risk of cardiac arrhythmia and thrombosis, as well as increasing peptic ulcers of the gastrointestinal tract. It diminishes the immune system's efficiency and leads to decreased levels of vitamins B and C.

As nicotine is an addictive drug, numerous withdrawal symptoms can occur on smoking cessation. These include the recurrence of headaches, bronchitis, nausea, palpitations, constipation, irritability and an increased appetite; nicotine usually deadens the taste buds and increases the blood sugar level.

An indication of the toxicity of nicotine is that 60 mg injected into a person's bloodstream is sufficient to kill him. A person who smokes 20 cigarettes a day ingests half the fatal dose.

Radioactive compounds

Polonium-210 and potassium-40 are carcinogenic radioactive compounds found in tobacco. Lead (Pb-210), bismuth (Bi-210) and polonium (Po-210) are long-lived radon daughters present in tobacco smoke. The shorter-lived radon daughters, such as those of tobacco smoke, are absorbed by aerosol particles in the atmosphere and can therefore be inhaled into the lungs. It is suspected that Pb-210 is present from radium-rich phosphate fertilisers and the adsorption of radon daughters on tobacco plant leaves.

Pesticides

Cigarette smoke contains a number of pesticides including DDT, dieldrin, endrin, parathion, endosulfan and paraquat.

Tar

When tobacco smoke cools in the mouth, it condenses to form tar. Tar is the substance that remains once nicotine and moisture are removed from tobacco. It contains poly aromatic hydrocarbons such as benzo(a)pyrene, pyrene, catechol, N-nitrosonornicotine, aromatic amines (e.g., 4-aminobiphenyl, 2 naphthylamine), alkenes and isoprenoids which give the flavour in smoke, nickel, arsenic, radioactive isotopes (e.g., 226Ra, 210Pb, 210Po), phenols, carboxylic acids, azaarenes, naphthenes and benzenes. Benzo(a)pyrene was discovered 30 years ago and is recognised as the most potent carcinogen in cigarette smoke. Arsenic, a carcinogen, is present in cigarette smoke. More tar is formed the faster the cigarette burns. Each cigarette produces between 0.5 and 35 mg of tar. The tar is deposited in the air passages of the lungs.

Formed from protein at temperatures greater than 700°C, hydrogen cyanide in cigarette smoke is converted to thiocyanate by the liver, kidney and intestines. This compound kills the cilia that clean out the lungs. Damaged and dead cilia are part of the well-known "smoker's cough." The respiratory cleaning system can no longer do its job; the violent spasmodic contraction necessary to eject waste is the definition of "smoker's cough."

The concentrations of cancer-causing nitrosamines in tobacco smoke are very high and 50 times higher in side stream than in mainstream smoke. These originate from nitric oxide, which is produced by tobacco smoke.

Health effects

Of the inhaled particles from cigarette mainstream smoke, 80 percent are deposited in the respiratory tract, notably the tracheobronchial region. Most of the SS smoke particles enter the lungs. Many of the health problems attributable to cigarettes are now known but the effects are often not visible until 20 to 30 years after an individual has started smoking.

Emphysema and bronchitis are two of the most common ailments of cigarette smokers. These are due to the presence of tar and cyanide gas in tobacco smoke. Emphysema is a condition that occurs when the walls of the air sacs in the lung break down. This reduction in the area of lung membrane reduces the ability of the lungs to absorb O_2 and release CO_2.

The carbon monoxide, nicotine and microfine particulates present in inhaled smoke are responsible for an increased risk of heart disease. Three of the more common problems are coronary heart disease (heart attacks, angina), peripheral vascular disease (blockages in legs) and cerebrovascular disease. In Australia alone, 800 limb amputations occur annually due to peripheral vascular disease caused by smoking.

Blood platelet function and lipid profiles are affected, often resulting in the condition atherosclerosis. The lining of arteries becomes narrow and rough and this, combined with blockages and clotting, leaves the blood unable to flow freely. When arteries become blocked, aneurisms result. Introducing even more danger, smoking increases the amount of stress chemicals such as catecholamines, cortisol and vasopressin.

Cancers

It is well known that smoking cigarettes causes cancer. Lung cancer is the most frequent cancer caused by smoking but cancers of the pharynx, mouth, oesophagus, pancreas and kidney also occur, and bladder and renal pelvic cancers can develop.

Lung cancer is the most common cause of death from cancer in industrial countries. The number of women dying from this is rapidly increasing. Squamous cell cancer is a common lung cancer of smokers and results in the destruction of cilia in the windpipe. Evidence indicates that the risk of lung cancer increases with the number of cigarettes smoked per day, duration of smoking, age at which smoking began, amount of inhalation and the tar and nicotine content of cigarettes. The presence of radon daughters, asbestos, uranium, nickel and other carcinogenic chemical compounds in the air with cigarette smoke increases the risk of lung cancer.

Tobacco smoke also has many negative synergistic effects. Alcohol and tobacco, while taken alone, produce about a threefold increase in the risk of mouth cancer; taken together this combination produces a fifteen-fold increase in risk. Female smokers using oral contraception increase their risk of heart and blood vessel disease, particularly if over thirty years old. Also, some drugs lose their effectiveness as a result of smoking. Tobacco smoke also acts synergistically with asbestos and radiation. Worldwide, more than three million people die each year due to tobacco smoking. But it doesn't have to be this way.

Yet another health effect caused by active or passive smoking is lower secretion of pancreatic juices, resulting in digestive system disorders. Other effects associated with smoking include migraines, pulmonary tuberculoses, gangrene, palmoplantar pustulosis (skin disorder), chronic sinusitis, peptic ulceration, upper respiratory tract infections, increased susceptibility to the flu and depletion of nutrients such as vitamins in the body. A form of blindness, known as tobacco amblyopia, can be attributed to heavy smoking.

Passive smoking

There is striking evidence that passive smoking causes lung cancer and that passive smokers may suffer the same chronic health effects as smokers. The US Surgeon General and US National Academy of Sciences report that the deaths of 20 percent of the 12,000 lung cancer deaths each year in the United States of America are due to passive smoking.

Acute health effects are also prevalent in passive smokers. Common symptoms include throat and eye irritation and headaches. The acrolein in smoke is a cause of eye irritation.

Children born to women who smoked during pregnancy suffer many adverse health effects. Benzo(a)pyrene, a known carcinogen, has been found to cross the placenta and enter foetal blood. Immune system depression can occur in a child exposed to smoke whilst in the womb or in his or her first years of life. The nicotine and carbon monoxide components of cigarette smoke are especially harmful to the foetus. When the nicotine passes into the mother's blood, it acts to constrict blood flow to the placenta and reduces the availability of oxygen and nutrients to the foetus. Nicotine also causes the release of the hormone oxytocin in the mother, which causes uterine contractions. The oxygen-carrying capacity of the blood of the smoker and also the foetus is reduced by carboxyhaemoglobin, which can result in tissue hypoxaemia. Studies have revealed that a baby's blood is very viscous if her mother smokes more than 20 cigarettes a day. The combined effect of CO and nicotine retard foetal growth; smokers' babies are usually born with a lower than average body weight and smaller-than-normal head circumference.

Children are susceptible not only when they are in the womb, but also when they are exposed to cigarette smoking in their early years. Nicotine can be passed to an infant through the mother's milk as the baby is breast-fed. Compared to adults, babies have a higher respiratory volume for their size and will inhale relatively large quantities of cigarette smoke. Research obtained by measuring the levels of cotinine in the saliva and urine of children suggested that a child who lived with parents who smoked 20 cigarettes a day would be exposed to the same amount of cigarette constituents as someone who smoked 90 cigarettes a year. It is not surprising, then, that many exposed children suffer from respiratory problems. The number of children suffering from wheezing, bronchitis, asthma, coughs and excess phlegm production increases with the incidence of parental smoking.

Parental smoking can be harmful or deadly to children. There is a strong association between smoking and Sudden Infant Death Syndrome (SIDS). Also reported are increases in the incidence of glue ear. Further, it has been shown that not only are the children of heavy smokers shorter on average than the children of non-smokers, but also their IQ levels are lower.

Smokers are also more likely to take longer to conceive and have premature births. The incidence of spontaneous abortion and foetal and neonatal death increases with smoking during pregnancy. Smoking is a significant factor in lowering conception rates of couples trying to get pregnant.

The politics of smoking

While all governments express concern about the increasing death and morbidity rates arising from tobacco use it is surprising to see that many governments, particularly in developed countries, continue to support the industry. For example, the EU spent 72 million Euros on a three-year campaign against smoking while subsidising its tobacco growers to the tune of one billion Euros. Many of the governments also derive an important income from the taxes on tobacco sales, but at what cost?

Australia is one of the leading nations in regard to cutting smoking rates. Some states have fallen behind as our politicians succumb to pressure from the hotel and tobacco lobby groups at the expense of our health and the health of our children. In one situation a prominent premier of NSW delayed and watered down the tobacco smoke control legislation in a particular state only to accept a lucrative directorship upon his retirement.

Fortunately, in Western Australia the monies raised from the sale of tobacco products go directly to Healthway to be used to subsidise sporting events that can no longer obtain corporate sponsorship from cigarette companies, or for the promotion of events that include anti-smoking messages. There are states with similar subsidies but the money from tobacco taxes goes directly to government coffers rather than to a separate health foundation.

With the rate of smoking declining in many of the Western countries, the large tobacco companies are searching for new markets to exploit in the Third World. However, many Third World countries have attempted to stop the movement of these tobacco companies and their highly sophisticated sales techniques into their countries, knowing the harm they will cause and the inability of the country to regulate the companies once they gain entry. The United States government has applied strong trade pressure on behalf of the cigarette companies for countries to open up, somewhat reminiscent of the beginning of the Boxer Rebellion when China was forced to buy opium. The conflicting attitudes of many Western governments send inconsistent messages to their people. Is it at all surprising, then, that many smokers reject government health promotion campaigns?

Every year, tobacco smoke causes the premature death of three million people. This is the equivalent of one person dying every 10 seconds. If current trends continue, this figure is estimated to increase dramatically to 10 million by 2020. In Australia alone, smoking results in more than 19,000 deaths each year.

PART FOUR

Chapter 13. Dust: What's in It, Anyway?

Particles

For most of us dust is a dirty word, but not a dangerous one. The worst it seems to do is make us sneeze. But if we studied common household dust under a microscope that could magnify by 10,000, what would we see? Things that are surprising, alarming and even disgusting. Dust is an aggregation of microscopic particles from diverse sources: organic, physical and chemical. Organic particles include pollens, insect body parts such as scales and hairs, human skin cells, dust mites and their faeces, mould spores, plant and animal debris including faeces, bacteria, viruses and even the eggs of various parasites. Physical particles include tiny grains of clay and sand (basically broken down rock) and minute particles of the many natural and synthetic compounds that we use in everyday life—asbestos fibres, paint, tile grout, plastic, carpet fibres, lead, glass, cement. Everything is breaking down into dust, including the human body. Chemical particles often "ride" on organic or physical dust—compounds such as pesticides, herbicides, insecticides, formaldehyde, solvents, xenooestrogens, phthalates and literally thousands of other chemicals. When you consider the fact that 3,000 new chemical compounds are developed each year and that the knowledge of their harmful effects lags well behind their introduction into the marketplace, dust begins to look less innocuous.

Dust particles vary in size from 10 microns (1,000 microns measure one millimetre) to less than 0.01 micron. Particles become respirable at 100 microns or less. The size of the particle determines how problematic it can be to our health. Those that lodge in the nose, pharynx and trachea are between 10 and 100 microns in size and are trapped by hairs and mucous. Particles between 2.5 and 10 microns are small enough to get into our tracheobronchial area and are again trapped by hairs and mucous. Particles of 2.5 microns and less can penetrate the alveoli, where gas exchange occurs between the lungs and bloodstream. Some particles will be identified as harmful and be dealt with by our white blood cells, while others will enter the blood capillaries. These contaminants interfere with the blood's capacity to carry oxygen and remove waste products. Some will be toxic to various organs and will accumulate in both organs and fatty tissue.

Dust particles of 0.01 micron sink through the air at a rate of approximately one metre in 140 days. The longer that microdust (particles of 10 microns or smaller) remains suspended, the more likely we are to breathe it. Particles from diesel fuel and some combustion particles can stay in the tracheobronchial region for as long as two years! On an ordinary day we breathe in about a teaspoon of microscopic particles.

Sources of particles

The dust in our homes includes particles from the outdoor air, by-products from combustion, particles created by people's activities, certain building materials and all the hundreds of products we bring into our homes. Levels of particulates are generally higher inside our houses than outside because they include the outdoor air levels plus the extra load of particles contributed from inside the house. Higher levels of dust are associated with our activities because we all have what is called a "personal activity cloud." This cloud of dust, in which we live, is generated by our activities—the dust that we are quite literally shedding all the time, and that which we activate. Remember the Peanuts character Pig Pen, who was perpetually surrounded by a cloud of dust? Our "halo" of personal dust is, of course, microscopic and invisible. Even a sedentary activity such as sitting at a computer will generate personal exposure to dust. Certain actions amplify our activity cloud. The disturbance we create when typing at a computer is amplified by the electric charge around the computer. Symptoms of this can be an itching feeling or itching eyes—good reasons to make sure that the area around the computer is as free of dust as possible.

All our actions will contribute to higher levels of particles inside but our personal exposure is higher if we are involved in activities such as cleaning, smoking, cooking (particularly if the food is burning!) brushing our hair or craft activities.

Particles from combustion

Combustion particles are mostly elemental carbon and act like tiny sponges, absorbing volatile organic compounds (VOCs) and heavy metals. They are mutagens and carcinogens and interfere with biochemical and neurological pathways.

Various sources of combustion pollute our homes, some from outside the house, others from inside. Outdoor combustion particles come from industrial smokestack emissions, vehicle exhausts, heating exhausts, forest fires and other open fires. Cars and lawnmowers running inside attached garages can be a source of particulates, as well as a source of deadly carbon monoxide. Homes located near major roads will usually have higher concentrations of fine particles from car exhausts. Because of the small size of some combustion particles, 0.1 micron or less in diameter, they can be seen only at very high concentrations. Sources of combustion particles inside our homes include heating appliances, cooking appliances and smoke.

Smoking

The single largest contributor of combustion particles inside the home is environmental tobacco smoke (ETS). In some cases, the particulates attributed to ETS comprise 50 to 90 percent of the total concentration of particulates. Tobacco smoke is a complex mixture of compounds, many of which are known or suspected carcinogens, such as polycyclic aromatic hydrocarbons (PAHs).

Carpets and dust contaminants

Carpets have many benefits: they insulate, reduce noise, are warm, soft on our feet, soften the contact of falls and can be easy to maintain. However, if not maintained properly, they can become a major source of particulates, accumulating dust from many sources and storing vast amounts of the stuff. This accumulated dust is activated and resuspended when it is disturbed. Our research has shown that most carpets are poorly maintained. Most vacuum cleaners used are of poor quality and there is a lack of understanding about how to properly clean and maintain both the carpet and the vacuum cleaner.

The distinction between cleaning and maintaining a carpet is important. Professional carpet cleaners use either hot water extraction (sometimes called steam cleaning) or dry cleaning, both of which are effective methods. Even with a very good vacuum cleaner, you initially require a minimum of three minutes per square metre to clean a carpet properly. Once the carpet has become conditioned, vacuuming time can be cut down to 30 seconds per square metre. The normal, superficial vacuuming done by most people is only maintaining the carpet. In many cases the vacuum cleaner is of such poor quality that it does not even achieve that.

There is a tendency for people to remove carpets in an attempt to reduce allergy problems such as asthma. While some people have reported positive effects, many people have not experienced improvements. There are no studies that show that removing carpet actually works in the case of asthma. While carpets accumulate dust, to a degree they also act to hold it down. However, inefficient cleaning of carpets does bring dust up to the surface where it can be redistributed.

Lead

Lead is often found as a contaminant in the dust in our homes, usually near the entrance where it is brought in on people's shoes. This contaminated dust will accumulate in carpets, where the possibility of it being ingested or being transferred to the skin is increased, especially if the dust particles are stirred. When we studied the amounts of lead in carpets we found the highest levels near the front door. The closer the house was to a busy road or a petrol station, the higher the level of lead.

Lead can cause very serious health problems, including damage to the nervous system, leading to behavioural changes and a decreased mental ability, inhibition of enzymes, interference with the growing foetus, colic, anaemia and kidney damage. Infants and young children are the groups most susceptible to lead exposure. Even at low levels, lead poisoning in children can cause IQ deficiencies, reading and learning disabilities, impaired hearing, reduced attention spans and hyperactivity and other behaviour problems. Pregnant women poisoned by lead can transfer lead to a developing foetus, resulting in adverse developmental effects.

While lead has slowly been removed from petrol over the past 20 years, it will remain as an environmental contaminant in the form of fine dust for many decades. Australia was one of the last developed countries to remove lead from petrol (almost 20 years after the USA). This was despite the toxic effects of lead being known as far back as the 1950s. Australia has an influential lead industry that has fought tooth and nail alongside the petrol industry and certain government departments to keep the lead in petrol. Shamefully, the health of the average person is usually not a consideration when weighed against the "health" of the economy when large amounts of money are at stake. The result of this reluctance to act means that many more Australians now have elevated levels of lead in their bodies and many children have been unnecessarily exposed to this toxic metal.

Dust from lead-based paints continues to pose a health problem. Although these paints were banned from indoor use decades ago, people with older homes are still being exposed to lead dust, another legacy of complacent governments. More than 80 percent of homes built before 1978 contain lead paint. It was the primary component (up to 40 percent) of white paint in Australia until the 1960s. In homes built before 1950, white lead-based paints were used as undercoats on interior and exterior timbers and walls and as a prime coat for troweled lath and plaster walls and cement rendered surfaces.

Small quantities of dust are continually produced from lead paint, settling on indoor surfaces. During periods of home renovation, there is an increase in the number of cases of lead poisoning reported. Researchers have found the household dust of recently renovated homes contains lead levels of 12,600 mg/m2. This is thousands of times higher than the normal background level.

In a recent incident, a family keen to renovate an older house was assured that the old paint on the outside of their home was not lead based. At the end of the first day of paint stripping, there was a layer of fine paint dust inside the home and in the new baby's room. Fortunately the mother listened to her intuition and had the dust tested. It was laden with lead. In this case the family acted quickly to avert potentially grave health problems. Have paint tested before you remove it if you think there may be a possibility of it being lead based. This is simple and inexpensive as the test kits are available from any reputable hardware or paint shop. Don't assume it will be fine. It is essential to test it and be sure.

Pesticides

Pesticides also accumulate in carpet to be released and inhaled, ingested or absorbed through the skin. Pesticides can be tracked in on shoes or carried in on your clothing and your skin. These chemicals also accumulate from indoor insecticide use. Aerosols such as fly spray and other insect sprays produce tiny droplets, which are directly inhaled by anyone in the room. Ultra-fine droplets float in the air for hours. The pesticides in "bombs," baits and powders can end up in your body. All pesticides are toxic, can contaminate your home and are likely to remain for months or even longer.

Pesticides used to control ants, cockroaches, silverfish, moths, flies, fleas and other pests adhere to microscopic dust particles where they can persist for long periods and later be released. Dirt on the soles of your shoes can be a major source of pesticides. If you apply pesticides to your garden, you are much more likely to have high levels of pesticides in your house dust. Research has shown that pesticides used for termite control, even when applied under the best possible conditions, persist for months and even years in house dust and indoor air.

Herbicides

Herbicides are toxic chemical compounds. If you apply herbicides to your garden you are more likely to have elevated levels of these chemicals inside your home. They can drift in from the outdoor air and will adhere to clothes and shoes. Even the "environmentally friendly" Roundup has breakdown by-products that can be detected for months after use. If you think you must use an herbicide to control weeds, don't use a spraying method of application, which allows the chemicals to become airborne, spreading them further and exposing you to greater contamination. Dabbing or painting applications offer better control of the chemical and reduce the amount you use. Even if you personally desist from using herbicides and pesticides, you may still unwittingly track them into your home from footpaths, verges, parks, playing fields, nature strips and other public spaces. This source of contamination is due to council spraying. Urge your local council and schools to operate with effective nontoxic alternatives, such as steam, to control weeds.

Allergens

Asthmatics are at a high risk from the allergens produced by animals (especially cats and dogs), dust mites (tiny creatures with impressive names such as Dermatophagoides pteronyssinus, Dermatophagoides microceras and Dermatophagoides farinae) and mould. Because these allergens float in the air, they are termed aeroallergens. Dust mites feed on mould and skin cells. Considering the amount of skin each of us sheds daily, we provide an ample source of food for these creatures. Dust mites are around two to 300 microns in length (slightly too small to be seen with the naked eye) and produce faeces measuring about 10 to 30 microns. The dust mite allergen comes from its digestive secretions and consequently the problem allergen, such as the protein Der p1, is contained in the dust mite's "poo." Like many other microorganisms, dust mites prefer humid and warm conditions. They are even able to absorb moisture from the air. Carpets and soft furnishings, including our pillows and beds, have their own microclimate, which is a little more humid than the surrounding air. Heated rooms with a constant temperature, along with the humid environment of soft furnishings and carpets, make perfect breeding grounds for these unwelcome houseguests.

Because of stable, warm temperatures, the provision of appropriate breeding areas and ample food, dust mite populations grow unchecked and their allergens may be a significant problem for many people. Mite infestations, as well as mould growth, can be reduced by lowering the inside humidity and allowing temperatures to fluctuate. Allow the house to heat up on hot dry days and to cool down on cold nights. Central heating, which provides a constant temperature, makes an ideal indoor climate for a mite population explosion.

At the risk of putting you off your bed altogether, we have to tell you that beds and pillows are dust mite heaven. The insulation of the bedding gives the mites protection from fluctuations in temperature. You would be amazed at the activity which begins beneath you when you lie down to rest at night—millions, even billions of mites migrate toward the surface of the mattress, drawn by the warmth and humidity generated by your body. Regularly vacuuming the pillow and mattress with an effective vacuum cleaner is helpful, but you will be relieved to know that dust mite covers are inexpensive, effective and obtainable from many chemists.

Heat is also an effective means of killing the biological "dust" that inhabits our carpets and other soft furnishings. The high temperatures used in properly conducted steam cleaning combat dust mites and mould effectively. The dust on wooden surfaces such as timber flooring was controlled in the old days by spreading wet tea leaves on the floor. While this probably did have advantages in reducing dust, people were also unknowingly controlling dust mite allergen, as the tannin in tea breaks down the Der p1. Nowadays most dust mite treatments contain a combination of tannin to break down the mite allergen and alcohol, which kills the dust mite itself.

Pet fur

Pet fur is a serious health problem for a large proportion of the population. Around 15 percent of allergy sufferers have positive reactions to cat and dog allergens. Rodent fur and bird feathers also contain allergens capable of causing reactions. Animal fur can carry other, smaller allergens into the respiratory system, compounding the sufferers' problems.

Pet fur is made more problematic by the ease with which it persists on surfaces and remains in carpet. Pet owners frequently carry the allergen around on their clothes. One study found cat allergen in an office at high enough levels to cause allergic reactions in some of the workers. The allergen had been brought in on a co-worker's clothes. The allergen was persistent, remaining active for months. Another study found that cinema seats were reservoirs for pet allergen.

Cat allergen

Cats produce a variety of allergens, the main one being Fel d1, which is secreted from their sebaceous glands. The size of cat allergen is less than 20 microns and can remain airborne for hours once disturbed.

Direct contact with Fel d1 can result in rapid onset of symptoms in allergy sufferers. Generally people seem to be more susceptible to cat allergens, with positive reactions to cats being twice as high as to dogs. Male cats secrete more Fel d1 than female cats but will secrete less once neutered. Some recent studies have given good news about animal allergens in that owning an animal, any kind of animal—be it a cat, a dog or even a cow—does seem to confer some protection against asthma. This appears contradictory, especially in the case of cats. There are also other positive effects from owing a pet. Pet owners generally tend to recover more quickly from illness, are usually more positive in outlook and generally live longer than non-pet owners.

Allergens of insect origin

There are also many allergens of insect origin, including their hair, faecal pellets and the decay of various body parts. Carpet beetles are microscopic insects that live off hair. They produce allergens and the larvae can cause itching. In the US, cockroach allergens appear to be a major contributor to the incidence of allergies in inner city areas. They do not yet appear to be a problem in Australia but perhaps we are simply not aware of it yet.

Chapter 14. Controlling Dust and Allergens

In general, the less dust on a surface, the less potential there is for redispersing the dust. A proper routine cleaning may eliminate or significantly reduce the amount of dust in "sinks" (reservoirs of dust, like soft furnishings), preventing the particles from being redispersed and therefore reducing exposure.

Four Steps to Managing Particulate Levels in Your Home

There are four basic strategies for reducing levels of indoor particulates:

1. Reducing the intake of particulates into the home;
2. Reducing the emissions of particulates from sources within the home;
3. Diluting airborne particulates by adequate ventilation; and
4. Removing particulates from indoor air.

If you use a combination of all of these techniques, you will reduce the particulate levels in your home significantly and enjoy better health as a result.

Vacuuming

Our research team has shown that the normal or conventional vacuum cleaners used by most households are not capable of removing large amounts of dust from carpets and are, in fact, capable only of removing the larger particles of dirt and debris— the visible dust. Even many of the commercial vacuum cleaners and so-called good residential vacuum cleaners remove only a small amount of the dust trapped within the carpet. Further, they do not remove larger grit particles trapped deep in the carpet, which cut the fibres and reduce a carpet's lifespan. This means that the carpet is not even being maintained, let alone cleaned.

Our research revealed that the low air flow (suction power) of conventional vacuum cleaners brought dust up to the surface of the carpet but failed to actually remove it, leaving it where it was easily stirred by movement. The efficiency of these vacuum cleaners is reduced even more as the bags begin to fill, resulting in a lower airflow and weaker suction. With such inefficient cleaning, dust particles gradually build up in the carpet, on furniture and in the air itself. This explains why some homes get dusty again far too soon after cleaning and why it never seems possible to keep them clean.

Poorly cleaned carpets have been specifically linked with tiredness, malaise and Sick Building Syndrome (SBS) symptoms, such as irritation of the eyes, airways and skin, as well as headaches and fatigue.

Our own research and a number of other studies found that airborne dust levels were reduced for long periods by up to almost 90 percent after vacuuming with an efficient filtration vacuum cleaner or after some other accredited method of professional carpet cleaning. There were also reductions in other airborne contaminants such as volatile organic compounds (VOCs) and allergen levels. Inefficient, conventional vacuum cleaners may actually be contributing to higher levels of suspended dust. This is not just because of their poor suction. They also have more porous dust bags (cloth bags being the worst offenders), allowing the microdust to pass into the exhaust airflow and to be redistributed. In fact, airborne dust levels during and directly after cleaning with these conventional models are two to 10 times greater in homes than before vacuuming! When you dust and then vacuum, a thin film of dust settles and becomes apparent on surfaces within an hour or so. Most of this comes from the dust redistributed by the vacuum, the rest from the activity at the time. Most vacuums, particularly those which have a bag type filter, suck at one end and exhaust out the other, releasing billions of microscopic particles which can float in the air for hours, waiting to be inhaled. These vacuum models may accurately be called "dust distributors." Their bags can provide a breeding ground for mould, which also exhausts into the air.

New vacuum models are continually coming onto the market, with better cleaning and filtration. This is a very positive step. Sometimes, however, extra filtration can lead to reduced airflow and weaker suction.

Choosing an effective vacuum

Many vacuum cleaner companies make exaggerated claims, which are not backed up by science, about their equipment. An important selling point is often the power of the motor. In the vacuums we tested, the power of the motor had little or no influence on the efficiency of the vacuum. In fact, it was the lowest powered motor that had the best results. It is the specific design of the motor and the vacuum that makes it many times more efficient. Other sales ploys include using a new vacuum with an empty bag and comparing it to your older machine. A new vacuum is going to outperform an old vacuum, especially if your machine's bag has not been emptied recently and if it has not had regular maintenance. A vacuum cleaner will perform much more efficiently if it is properly maintained. Only one in every 200 people actually get their vacuum serviced, yet it is necessary to maintain it, just as we would a car or any other piece of important equipment.

Our research has shown the best vacuuming systems have a cyclonic/centrifugal action, with multi-level filtration capable of removing particle matter down to 0.2 micron in size. The cyclonic/centrifugal motion spins the various dirt sizes out of the airstream before it flows through the final filter. This ensures that the suction is not reduced because dirt does not clog up the filter. These models may incorporate an activated carbon or charcoal filter for removing pollutants such as VOCs and odours. They also have an attachment called a mechanical beating head or turbo head for vacuuming soft surfaces. Its special action is critical for picking up and removing the dirt from carpets, including deeply engrained dirt. Two systems that stand out here are Filter Queen and Dyson vacuums.

Central vacuum systems can be effective but must be fitted with a high quality filter. The motor and filter should not be inside the building, nor should they be located in an area frequently used to access the house, such as an attached garage. The noise generated by the motor can be a problem.

Vacuums with water filters are often overrated. They pass the vacuumed air through a compartment of water that removes most of the dust. However, many microdust particles pass through the water either in bubbles or because they do not dissolve readily. Just as the bag filters need changing, the water needs to be renewed as it becomes dust laden. Emptying and cleaning the water compartment is very important, as it can become a breeding ground for microorganisms. Water filled vacuums are also heavier and a little more awkward to use.

The use of a high efficiency vacuum fitted with a HEPA (High Efficiency Particle Attenuator) filter significantly reduces the amount of suspended indoor dust, as a HEPA microfilter is capable of trapping most of the microdust. A good vacuum cleaner sales person will know a HEPA filter. The HEPA filter alone does not guarantee quality of cleaning, rather it guarantees cleaner air during cleaning. If not maintained regularly, HEPA vacuums will also become "dust distributors." We have seen many vacuums with HEPA filters that have an accumulation of dust on the outside of the filter, which means it is no longer functioning efficiently and that the seals need to be replaced.

How to vacuum effectively

Our research has also shown that technique, as well as equipment, is important. Most vacuuming quickly brushes over the surface of the carpet to remove the visible dirt and fluff but fails to remove the deeply ingrained dirt tangled in the carpet pile. The longer you vacuum in one place, the more dust and grit you will remove. Vacuuming in one place for a minute every six weeks is more effective than vacuuming that spot every week for 10 seconds. Even if you have a good cyclonic vacuum cleaner, to clean hygienically it will still take this amount of time. If you have a vacuum with a bag filter it will take double the time. However, cleaning this way keeps down the amount of microdust in the air for months.

One of our studies was conducted in an office building, where we replaced normal, conventional vacuum cleaning equipment with a high efficiency vacuum using HEPA filtration. The result was a more efficient removal of dust from surfaces, which significantly reduced airborne dust and also lowered the number of health complaints in the building. People reported fewer symptoms associated with Sick Building Syndrome. Not only did they feel better, but also because of the improved standard of cleaning they felt more positive about their work environment and became more productive. The economic benefits of cleaning impressed the company so much that they initiated healthy cleaning practices based on our research.

If these principles are adopted at home, you will actually find your cleaning is more efficient and economical and your family's health will benefit. Let's say you vacuum two hours a week using a poor quality vacuum—a "dust distributor." You not only pollute the air but also have to clean twice as frequently. You could halve your effort by using efficient equipment, saving labour, time and money.

Rugs are an alternative to carpets, but they also need to be regularly cleaned and maintained. Taking rugs outside and shaking them and putting them in the sun and occasionally washing them are all suitable treatments. In Scandinavia and Northern Europe it is customary to take the rugs down to the river and wash them in summer. In fact, it is a social event and there are long racks for hanging up the rugs once they have been rinsed. In winter, they are thrown into the snow, shaken down and then brought back inside. Not as socially satisfying, but still very effective. Australia has the advantage of receiving long hours of sunlight and ultraviolet light is a very effective sterilising agent. Put your rugs out into full sunlight and turn them over after a couple of hours. Then shake, beat or vacuum thoroughly. This should be done every three months or at the very least twice a year. You should also do it with your pillows and doonas. It is what our grandparents did and is still an effective way of cleaning and sterilising our bedding.

Professional carpet cleaning

Professional carpet cleaning should be done on all carpets every six to 12 months. However, as in every industry, there are contractors who are thorough and professional and those who do more harm than good. We have found that some carpet cleaners with very cheap rates leave behind more contaminants than were there prior to cleaning and that they damage the carpet as well. The money would have been better spent getting the job done properly. Thorough cleaning will increase the life of your carpet, not shorten it. The highest level of professional carpet cleaning is achieved through the Australasian Carpet Cleaning Industry (ACCI). The ACCI trains the best cleaners and, to retain membership, training needs to be continually updated. The ACCI has recently introduced an advanced level of training for 100 ACCI members through our scientific principles of cleaning, known as the Health and Environmental Cleaning System (HECS). To have the most effective carpet cleaning, contact an accredited HECS technician.

Chemical cleaning

Using chemicals to clean carpets can have deleterious health effects. Chemical cleaners, fungicides and acaricide (a pesticide used to kill dust mites and their eggs) contain many toxins that can cause headaches and other health symptoms. Residues of these chemicals are left behind in the carpet and will also attach to respirable dust.

While we don't want to dwell on cleaning chemicals we recently surveyed 425 homes and found that 16 percent of people who do the cleaning at home react to cleaning chemicals. The most frequent symptoms included skin complaints, irritation of the nose and throat and respiratory problems, including asthma. However, perhaps of greatest concern was the fact that the majority, 84 percent, thought chemicals did not pose a health risk and only 33 percent regularly read the labels and instructions! It was only those who were adversely affected who recognised a problem. This demonstrates today's prevalent attitude about chemicals: "If it's not affecting me now, it's OK."

This mindset was the downfall of an older lady who now reacts to many cleaning chemicals. In the past she thought people who complained of chemical sensitivities were "whiners," until she began to be affected herself. This woman has now been forced to make enormous changes in order to manage her own chemical sensitivities. Her understanding that many household cleaning agents contain toxic substances came at the price of her health.

Cleaning products contain a cocktail of chemicals. They should be used sparingly, if at all, and always stored in a safe place. Mixing cleaning chemicals together is very hazardous. For example, mixing bleach with an ammonium disinfectant "to make it more effective" creates the very toxic chloramine and chlorine gas, which is a major cause of adult poisoning in the home. While most people recover during the 24 hours following exposure, some will suffer from long-term health problems.

The most positive response in our survey was the fact that a large percentage of householders reported a willingness to spend more money for safer chemicals.

Another of our surveys revealed that the average home has 20 to 40 different cleaning agents. These can be reduced to six or less. Don't be seduced by advertisements that say you need more chemicals to clean effectively and hygienically. What did our grandparents use? Usually bicarb soda, borax, vinegar, soap and water. These simple, cheap and relatively nontoxic substances are still effective cleaning agents.

Chapter 15. Dusting Hard Surfaces

Hard floors are of benefit in rooms that are likely to have a lot of activity or heavy traffic. Like carpets, they must also be properly maintained; as hard surfaces don't trap particles in the way that carpet fibres do, accumulated dust is more easily disturbed. How we clean hard surfaces is important, whether it be a bench top or flooring. The best strategy is to use the new fibre technology or the vacuum system we have already discussed.

Fibre cleaning is based on early research that found that certain fibres are able to lock in dust particles better than others. Ostrich feathers are famous for picking up dust because of the unique, microscopic arrangement of their quills. Other feathers don't have this unusual characteristic and, as a result, most commercial feather dusters will only disperse dust into the air and make it available for you to inhale. Most cloth dusters do the same and should be relegated to the bin. The use of old clothes as dusters is even worse, as they create more dust than they remove. Even wetting them is ineffective, as they will still generate airborne dust.

The majority of people rarely think about airborne dust when cleaning—they are satisfied as long as the surface looks clean when they finish. Little do they realise that the dust soon settles to re-contaminate the surface. Even more importantly, their "dusting" has now become harmful as the microdust, which will remain suspended for hours, even days, can now be inhaled. Ask any asthmatic. We breathe many thousands of litres of air each day, so if the air we breathe is dust laden, we quickly accumulate microdust in our lungs. Most of us would be repelled by the idea of eating or licking directly off a surface such as a kitchen bench or floor, yet we readily accept breathing in contaminated air laden with dust and chemicals. While surface hygiene is important, air hygiene is equally important, if not more so.

Fibre technology

Fibre technology works in three ways. Fibre tips are able to break down grease particles into smaller particles. The point of the fibre tip lifts dirt and grease off the surface and the charge of static electricity between fibres helps collect it. Once the particles are in the cloth, the physical structure and the charge of static electricity "locks in" the dust. (If the cloth is rubbed on a computer or TV screen before using it for the first time, this static charge is increased.) The surface area of the fibres is extremely large, enabling large volumes of dust to be held in the cloth. At the microscopic level, all surfaces are uneven, even smooth glass bench tops. The fibres are engineered to be different lengths so they can reach into the pockets of uneven surfaces, "scoop out" the dust and trap it. Different fibre technology cloths are specialised for different tasks. To clean the cloths, just wash them.

Perhaps the worst cleaning method is the wet bucket and mop. Not only does it increase airborne levels of bacteria but also it leaves behind even higher levels of bacteria on the "cleaned" surface. Even a sponge mop treated with an antibacterial solution did not deliver a better result than microfibre cleaning technology when the number of bacteria left on the surface was measured.

Our research into Enjo fibre technology has shown that fibre cloths reduce surface dust and dirt and do not contribute to airborne dust and microorganisms such as fungi or bacteria. Our most recent study has shown that fibre technology provides the best bench cleaning cloth, removing 99.99% of bacteria on all surfaces, even a rough surface, such as Formica, which is difficult to clean. By contrast, the other dry and wet methods of dusting often generate large volumes of airborne dust containing bacteria and fungi. The person cleaning gets a good dose of dust and the microdust stays in the air for hours, weeks, or months for others to breathe it, too.

In our study it was the generic brand anti-bacterial cloths and sponges that performed the most poorly. Some contained very high levels of bacteria, which were left on the "cleaned" surfaces. We found that there were no advantages in using antibacterial cloths or sponges and several disadvantages. People think that they are protected by the antibacterial agents and are less inclined to rinse them thoroughly. Antibacterial agents also add to the chemical burden in the home. Whatever type of bench wipe you use in the kitchen, rinse it in hot water before and after you use it, then allow it to dry. A big tip is not to allow it to remain damp. The same goes for your soap. Don't keep it in a soap dish with a pool of water.

Fibre technology is also environmentally sound in that the product is made to last and largely manufactured from recycled, synthetic fibre. The cloths themselves can be continuously recycled. Because none or very little cleaning chemical is needed with fibre technology, this cleaning method reduces the use of chemical cleaning agents, even dishwashing detergents.

We recently conducted a study in homes where fibre cleaning technology was used. The results showed that 75 percent less cleaning chemicals were used than in homes using traditional methods. This is a saving of hundreds of dollars over the course of a year and is better for the environment. Less chemicals in the home reduces the possibility of poisoning, being affected by long-term chemical exposure or becoming chemically sensitised. People using fibre technology reported that they spent less time cleaning but considered their homes cleaner and safer than before.

Our research has shown that by purchasing the correct equipment you can have a cleaner home or office building with less effort and save money. Good equipment and an understanding of the science of cleaning can cut cleaning time and costs by 25 to 30 percent.

The key point we wish to make is that dust is a serious health hazard. We need to revolutionise our thinking and begin cleaning for health rather than aesthetics. The cleaning methods you use can be the best preventative medicine in your home or its biggest polluter. An inefficient system may keep your house or office looking "clean" but is actually continually compromising your health.

Preventative measures: shoes and mats

Reducing the intake of particles into buildings is perhaps the best strategy but often the least practiced. Significant amounts of external dust are tracked in on our shoes. Our research has shown that removal of shoes at the door and the use of walk-off mats to prevent tracked in soil will reduce indoor dust levels in offices and homes. We found up to 50 percent less airborne microdust in houses where shoes were removed before entering, as compared to homes without this practice. This is an easy and effective means of reducing dust, it costs nothing and it reduces the need to clean.

Specially designed mats are also effective for removing microdust from shoes but they need to be walked on for six to nine steps to be effective. One short mat at the door entrance is not likely to reduce indoor dust unless people stand and wipe their feet. Brushing your shoes before entering the house is another effective practice. In many public places overseas there are shoe brushes on which you can quickly rub your shoes, removing much of the dust and grime from both soles and uppers.

We suggest a pair of slippers or other footwear that is never worn outside become your indoor shoes. Wearing a pair of dripping, mud-caked work boots indoors is accepted as unclean and we need to extend this thinking to our normal shoes, which carry in toxic dust.

Cleaning for health rather than for cosmetics means reducing and controlling indoor dust. Awareness about the hazards of dust and biological contaminants means we also know just what it is we are cleaning and why. We need to invest in our health by buying vacuums that comply with the suction and filtration standards required for healthy cleaning. We need to stop using poor quality dusters and mops that resuspend dust and we need to apply cleaning and maintenance strategies that stop the growth of microorganisms and moulds.

Last, but not least, we must cut down on the amounts of cleaning chemicals we use or replace them with safer alternatives, such as the simple products our grandparents used, or microfibre technology which cleans hygienically and does not require cleaning agents.

Chapter 16. Asbestos and Mineral Particulates

Mineral particulates often found in the indoor air include asbestos, carbon, clay and synthetic mineral fibres. Generally, mineral particulates come from indoor sources and they may be brought through ventilation systems, shoes and clothing.

Asbestos has a fibrous nature with a high tensile strength and excellent resistance to heat, abrasion and chemical reaction. It is the only natural mineral fibre that can be woven into a fireproof fabric. It is because of these properties that asbestos has been used extensively in all areas of manufacturing and industry. This use was so widespread that many homes, schools and buildings now contain asbestos in some form or another.

Three types of asbestos are used commercially:

- Chrysotile (white asbestos)

- Crocidolite (blue asbestos)

- Amosite (brown or grey asbestos)

The unique properties of asbestos and its toxic effects have been known for more than 100 years. Asbestos was identified at the turn of the 20th century as a source of occupational illness.

The first case of asbestos-related disease reported in Britain was in 1899. By the early 1940s, asbestos was an identified occupational lung carcinogen. Despite this early knowledge, we continued, and still continue, to use asbestos products. The thousands of people who have died and are dying of asbestos-related diseases is a direct result of government and industry inaction for, despite the fact that it was known for at least 50 years to be a deadly material, asbestos was still mined. Numerous studies have proven asbestos to be carcinogenic. It is a health risk confined not just to those working directly with it, although this certainly increases the risk of illness. A recent legal case found a woman was exposed to deadly asbestos fibres simply by handling her husband's work clothes.

The toxicity of asbestos is directly related to its physical structure. While asbestos in itself is not a toxin as it is chemically inert, the inhalation of asbestos fibres causes disease and death. The hazards of exposure are directly related to the degree to which these fibres "slough" off asbestos products and the amount of asbestos dust inhaled. Inhaled particles less than eight microns can reach the alveoli. Because most asbestos particles have a diameter of three microns or less, their potential to reach the very smallest recesses of the lungs is great.

Chrysotile (white asbestos) fibres are not straight but spiral in shape and usually hit the sides of the peripheral bronchial airways and air spaces. Although they penetrate the lung tissue, they can be removed from the respiratory system by normal physiological processes.

Crocidolite (blue asbestos) produces long, thin, straight fibres, often less than 0.1 micron in diameter. Because they are so thin, crocidolite fibres tend not to fall out of the inhaled air as it flows into the lungs. Instead they align themselves in the centre of the airflow, allowing them to penetrate deeply.

Amosite (brown asbestos) fibres are different again in shape and size. Because they can be trapped by the hairs and mucous that protect our respiratory system, they are less damaging.

Health problems related to asbestos

The major health problems caused by asbestos are:

1. Large amounts of scar tissue are laid down in the lungs in the years following exposure, causing irreversible damage to the lung tissue. Oxygen absorption is impaired and with further exposure the increasing amounts of scar tissue make the lungs stiff, less elastic.

2. Lung cancers caused by the inhalation of asbestos fibres include tumours of the bronchial tubes and the alveoli. These cancers have a long latency period, taking 20 years or longer to develop. People who smoke and have also been exposed to asbestos are particularly prone to developing lung cancer. Their chance of dying from lung cancer is increased many times when compared to a non-smoking person - even one who has been exposed to asbestos.

3. Other cancers include carcinomas of the larynx, abdomen and bowel. Although limited study has been conducted on ingestion of asbestos fibres, scientists and doctors have linked the fibres to cancers of the colon and peritoneum.

4. Mesothelioma is a rare cancer of the outer membrane covering the lung (the pleura). Few patients survive more than 18 months from the time of diagnosis, as the disease is usually well advanced due to its long latency period. Crocidolite (blue) asbestos is the most potent agent in producing this cancer because

of the size and shape of its fibres. Studies here and abroad have also shown that mesothelioma can be contracted after only short exposure to low levels of blue asbestos dust. Western Australia leads the world in the number of mesothelioma cases reported per year, with cases here expected to reach as high as 7,000 over the next few years, peaking in 2020.

Asbestos is ubiquitous in our environment and most of us carry many fibres in our lungs. This was confirmed by studies during the 1980s on people who had not been occupationally exposed to asbestos. About one in five mesothelioma cases appears not to be related to exposure through direct contact at work.

Removing asbestos

Almost all pre-1984 buildings, including schools, contain asbestos in some form. Routine repairs, maintenance and renovation of these buildings can release fibres into the air. There is strong, informed opinion that removal of asbestos is not the first or only option. Removing asbestos may pose a higher risk to health and may cost more than other treatments, which do not risk disturbing and releasing the fibres. However, removal will need to occur at some time. The question is when should it be done?

Removing asbestos from your home

If you have asbestos in your home and are opting for removal, make sure that you employ professionals who are experienced in asbestos removal. Some companies employ sub-contractors who are not properly trained and do not understand the risks involved. In Western Australia, asbestos removal and disposal is covered under Occupational Health and Safety regulations and legislation. Contractors should comply with these regulations. The health department or Department of Occupational Health and Safety in your state will be able to provide you with a copy of pertinent regulations. Obtain these before you talk to your contractor. Ask to see the contractor's safety procedures in writing. They should be included in the contract you will be asked to sign. Disposal may come under the authority of the Department of Environmental Protection. Only certain waste disposal sites will accept asbestos and there is usually a fee charged.

Australia currently imports 1,700 tonnes of raw asbestos each year and 1.5 million products containing asbestos. Our largest use of asbestos is in automotive brakes, clutches and other friction products. Because the majority of these are used in automobiles, there is no control of the fibres once these products are distributed and used. Fibres are released into the environment as a vehicle's brake linings or clutch plates wear down; these particles become part of the microscopic dust on our streets. About 75 percent of asbestos used in Australia is chrysotile with the remaining 25 percent being crocidolite or amosite.

Synthetic fibres

Synthetic mineral fibres (SMFs) or man-made mineral fibres (MMMFs) include ceramic fibres, fibreglass and rockwool. The various SMFs are made from different materials and by various manufacturing techniques, leading to diverse characteristics in both performance and health effects.

Synthetic mineral fibres have long been recognised as a cause of irritation to the skin, eyes and the upper respiratory tract. Studies on workers exposed to SMFs in the manufacturing of rockwool and slagwool have shown a significant increase in deaths from lung cancer. There is a suggestive, but not significant, increase in cases of lung cancer in workers exposed to small-diameter fibres in the manufacture of glasswool.

Fibreglass (glass filament) has become a concern because of its widespread use as a substitute for the now largely abandoned asbestos. The risk posed by fibreglass is disputed. Studies on glass fibres have not demonstrated a cancer risk. Most glass filaments have a diameter of between five and 15 microns and only fibres less than three microns are able to enter deep into our lungs. However, the resin coating of fibreglass is phenol formaldehyde, which in many countries is classified as a human carcinogen. Although conclusive epidemiological evidence of lung cancer caused by fibreglass inhalation is lacking, lung diseases similar to those caused by asbestos have been evident in some studies.

Recently, the fibreglass and insulation industries have developed a degradable form of fibreglass that has no demonstrated carcinogenic potential because of the way in which it breaks down. The three major manufacturers of fibreglass insulation in Australia now produce this biosoluble insulation under the code fbs1 (fibre biosoluble 1).

Insulation

"Which insulation should I use?" is a frequently asked question. Several years ago we would have said wool or paper (cellulose) fibre, but after personal experience with wool and hearing from a number of people who have had problems with the paper fibre, our recommendation is biosoluble fibreglass. You may also wish to consider recycled cloth insulation—some companies are using recycled blue jeans to make home insulation. Whichever insulation you choose, make sure that it is laid on top of a barrier and not loose when put in the roof space. It should be installed in segments and covered. You should not be able to see the insulation from any position inside a room. If fibres are visible, the barrier has not been laid down properly during installation.

When we think of microorganisms we usually think of infection causing bacteria, or bacterial food poisoning or viruses such as influenza. We rarely think of the hundreds of different types of biological particles that circulate in the air around us - the complex 'aeroflora' and 'bioaerosols'. Airborne bacteria, viruses, pollen and fungi, along with their spores, and other 'dust' of biological origin are found both outdoors and indoors. The indoor environment often provides very favourable conditions for proliferating microorganism growth and concentrating their populations inside buildings.

Bioaerosols affect people's health in quite different ways to those of their chemical counterparts. Biological particulates may be of plant origin such as pollen, spores and moulds, or animal origin such as bacteria, viruses, insect hair, dust mite allergen, insect body parts and waste products (faeces). These bio-contaminants have been associated with serious adverse health effects such as allergies, infectious diseases, respiratory problems and hypersensitive reactions.

Microorganisms and their by-products may be the cause of 'sick building syndrome' (SBS) in cases where no other particular cause has been found. In fact bio-contaminants have been associated as the primary causal agents in 35% to 50% of cases where buildings have been classified with SBS. Respiratory infections alone account for some 50-60% of all community acquired illness. The transmission of certain infectious diseases is more readily achieved indoors than outdoors and the likelihood of transmission is greater in airconditoned buildings than those using natural ventilation. The transmission of human diseases such as influenza, measles, rubella, chicken pox and rhinovirus infection is especially enhanced in crowded and poorly ventilated indoor environments, such as classrooms, pubs and night clubs. Recycling the indoor air through air conditioning systems which are ineffective or not properly maintained assists the spread of disease.

Factors assisting microorganism growth

All microorganisms have basic requirements for growth: high humidity, appropriate temperatures and a physical and nutritional medium on which to reproduce. All of these requirements are frequently provided indoors. Temperatures between 25°C and 45°C are optimal, but temperatures above 70°C cause microorganisms to die. A suitable, nutrient-rich medium such as dust, dirt or decomposing rubber enables them to flourish.

Many modern appliances with their uncleaned, stagnant water reservoirs provide ideal conditions for the growth of microorganisms. These include air conditioners, humidifiers, cooling towers, vapourisers, nebulisers, cold-mist vapourisers, spas, hot tubs, self-defrosting refrigerators, clothes dryers and some storage hot water systems (those that don't maintain temperatures above 70°C). Showers, bathrooms, flush toilets, basements and other areas prone to periodic humidity or leaking, also provide friendly environments for micro-organisms. Even respiratory equipment that has been rinsed in tap water containing these microorganisms poses a risk. Materials such as fabrics, carpets, leather, wood, paint, paper, greases, oils, soaps, pastes and plants all provide optimal conditions for microbial growth when moistened.

In our work we have identified two serious problem areas: air conditioning systems that are not cleaned or maintained, and carpets which have had water damage and have not dried out properly.

Organisms infecting the respiratory system can be transmitted in airborne droplets (i.e., in spray from coughing or sneezing) or on dust particles. Droplets are the smallest particles, between 10 and 2 microns. They contain bacterial and viral residues from larger particles expelled by coughing, sneezing and talking, and are able to remain airborne for long periods.

Bacteria

Most bacteria are non-pathogenic, that is, they do not cause diseases. These bacteria are beneficial to us, essential for our internal health and the health of our environment. The task of distinguishing the harmful from the harmless is difficult, given the huge number of similar species which co-exist in even a small part of our environment.

Legionella is well known as an indoor, airborne disease. Sporadic and epidemic Legionella infections occur regularly. As many as 116,000 cases occur annually. The majority of Legionella infections are due to bacterial contamination in air conditioner water cooling towers. The bacteria are released in droplets from the towers, sucked into the system and then spread throughout the building. Domestic air conditioning systems which allow water to settle may also become a breeding ground for the Legionella bacteria. Legionella is present in the air and on surfaces, including soil, but the concentrations are too low to cause a problem. Only when it finds the ideal conditions in some pooled water and a means of distribution does it become deadly. Water towers must be monitored and treated regularly. This is a legal requirement under both state and federal legislation throughout Australia.

A lesser known source, but responsible for an increasing number of cases, is inhalation of the dust from composted and bagged soil conditioners. The product is packed in plastic bags which retain the moisture, and they are often stored in a warm place, such as direct sunlight. When the bag is opened, micro-dust is released and inhaled. Piercing the bag (avoid inhaling!) and leaving it to breathe before fully opening it will go someway in reducing the amount of micro-dust, but care should still be taken. Contamination of these products is becoming more widespread, but the actual extent of contamination is unknown. Warnings are now printed on the bags, but it is entirely up to the consumer to take protective action - so take care.

Hospital infections

Hospital caused or 'nosocomial' infections are a major problem in hospitals around the world. Pathogenic bacteria that were relatively easy to contain with standard infection controls are now extremely difficult to control due to the misuse and overuse of antibiotics. This has occurred not only with prescribed antibiotics for humans but with the wide spread use of antibiotics in animal farming. Antibiotic resistant species include methicillin resistant Staphylococcus aureus (MRSA), glycopeptide resistant Enterocci, and multiple antibiotic resistant Mycobacterium tuberculosis (MDR TB). More resistant species are being identified every year. Once antibiotic resistant organisms become established, the issues of cross infection control and elimination can not only seriously disrupt the day to day operation of a hospital but also lead to loss of life and disabling illnesses.

In the USA approximately 10% of patients now acquire such an infection during their hospitalisation. Over 2 million people are affected each year and the cost to the health sector is over $4.5 billion annually. These infections account for 50% of all hospital complications. In 1996 in Australia it was estimated that 18,000 patients died as a direct result of their hospital care (how many deaths were due to infections is not known) while 50,000 people suffered permanent disability because they were infected while they were in hospital. Most people know of an example of such cases, like the resistant pseudomonas infection contracted by Peter's nephew went he went in for removal of an ingrown toenail. It was 6 months before the infection was brought under control. Another example involves a friend who contracted both pseudomonas and golden staff infection after surgery due to a motor bike accident. A year and a half later, the infection in the injured leg, which now has a metal plate, was finally brought under control with the use of colloidal silver.

In the UK it is estimated that nosocomial infections result in 950,000 lost bed days in acute hospital care, at a financial cost of 111 million pounds per year.

Although it is likely that hospital staff, primarily by hand carriage, are the main vehicle of cross infection, the role of inanimate, environmental sources is also being recognised as a source of cross-contamination. More recent research shows that pathogenic microorganisms are widespread in the environment and inanimate objects are a likely source of cross contamination. As far back as 1983, MRSA was identified as being ubiquitous in the environment, including the air, on elevated surfaces and floor surfaces. Mattresses were identified as the source of an outbreak of pseudomonas in 1980. Any movement in a room is likely to make tens of thousands of these infectious micro-organisms airborne, where they can spread to all surfaces, including the human body. The blankets that are spread over patients at night may be a major source of contamination.

Pillows, mattresses and privacy curtains are also likely reservoirs. The surfaces of bathroom taps and door handles can present very high concentrations of infectious organisms.

Improved hygiene practices such as hospital staff washing their hands before contacting each patient helps to reduce the likelihood of spreading infection, although this measure has not succeeded in helping the hundreds of thousands of people who contract infections in hospitals and nursing homes every year. Nor does it help the individuals for whom these infections prove fatal every year.

Although exact death and infection rates are not known, the severity and seriousness of the problem is increasing. Antibiotics are becoming less and less effective in controlling the superstrains of bacteria we ourselves have helped to produce through the overuse of 'wonder drugs'. Antibiotics have often been inappropriately prescribed for minor infections, for viral infections or simply because the patient expects a prescription. Another concern is the non-therapeutic use of antibiotics in intensive animal farms (in this context euphemistically called 'growth promotants') such as in poultry and pork production. Antibiotics are added to the animals' feed to make them gain weight faster, increasing production. As yet, there is little science to show that this practice is definitely linked to the development of 'super strains', but it is a likely and very serious possibility. Although many European countries have now banned this practice, Australia still allows the use of 'growth promotants' in animal feed.

Food poisoning.

Around 4 million Australians are affected by food poisoning every year. Of these poisonings, 80% have been traced to the food industry - the result of reheating food or poor storage. Food which is gently heated becomes a breeding ground for micro-organisms and in a few hours can contain many millions of bacteria. Warming left over food from the previous day or even just eating it cold can be a major source of contamination in homes. Benchtops and kitchen surfaces need to be thoroughly cleaned. No food scraps or water should remain. Water is the most critical ingredient, as bacteria love moisture. Another major source of contamination can be created by using the same utensils for preparing different foods. Separate knives and cutting boards should be used for meat and vegetables and for cooked and raw food, or the utensils washed thoroughly in hot water between their preparation.

Kitchen wipes also become a breeding ground for bacteria. Rinse them well in hot water a few times before wiping a bench or food surface, and hang them where they will dry out while not in use. Our research shows that antibacterial cloths are not really necessary and do not provide much benefit over thorough hot water rinsing.

Two of the most common forms of food poisoning are from Campylobacter and Salmonella bacteria.

Viruses are quite different to bacteria in that they require a living host cell in order to replicate. Every known animal, plant or microbial cell is able to be infected by at least one type of virus. Viruses undergo genetic variation regularly and are able to 'outwit' the host's defences. Many viruses are transmitted via droplets from coughing and sneezing, and may stay suspended in the air for considerable periods, making viral infection common and repetitive.

The size of viral particles means they are very difficult to control indoors. Isolation of the infected person to reduce transmission is probably the most practicable solution. Viruses such as chicken pox and measles are transmitted in seasonal patterns by airborne, breath-vapour droplets. With the coming of winter, people congregate indoors and infection spreads quickly, particularly if there is recirculated air from air conditioning systems. Unless there is a secondary bacterial infection antibiotics are unnecessary in the treatment of viral infections such as influenza.

Chapter 18 Mould

Moulds are perhaps the most opportunistic of the micro-organisms, and are found virtually everywhere, indoors and outdoors. They thrive wherever there is the least bit of moisture and nutrition – in fact they are tiny, enzyme-producing and cellulose-eating factories. There is a mould for every occasion and almost every material. They work continually on organic materials, breaking them down. Moulds are vital in the process of decomposition and recycling of organic material, and are essential and beneficial for life. Indoors, however, where their populations can concentrate, moulds become a problem.

Fungi are the most frequent cause of biodegradation of building materials. This 'biocorrosion' happens to building materials such wood, chipboard and plaster as organic and inorganic acids are released from the fungi. This is not surprising as fungi are capable of breaking down rock in nature. Ideal conditions for fungi growth are damp, humid conditions. In recent years the opportunity for growth of fungi and hence mycotoxin release has increased with increased flooding and thermal modernisation of residential buildings. Allergies and mycotoxicosis can be caused by extended periods of mould exposure.

Mould growths can often be seen in the form of discolouration, ranging from white to orange and from green to black, and present many textures, including slimy, powdery and hairy.

Moulds have diverse effects on our health due primarily to their production of spores and toxins, some of which are VOCs. Symptoms caused by moulds range from allergies to liver cancer. Mould can also cause conditions such as SBS and skin infections. It is inadvisable for anyone to live or work in a mouldy indoor environment.

Much of the mould found indoors comes from outdoor sources. It is common to find mould spores in indoor air and growing on damp surfaces. Everyone is exposed to mould on a daily basis without evident harm. The spores are tiny and readily airborne. Their dispersal is assisted in the indoor environment by air conditioners, humidifiers and human activity. When inhaled in large numbers they cause health problems. The vulnerability of an individual varies greatly, and depends upon the nature of the mould material (allergenic, toxic, or infectious), the amount of exposure, and the susceptibility of the exposed person. Some spores are allergens and may trigger a full allergic response if the person is susceptible, causing symptoms such as red and watery nose and eyes, coughing, sneezing, itching, lowered blood pressure, rapid and strained breathing and increased heart rate. In severe cases anaphylactic shock may occur, which is fatal without immediate medical assistance.

Mycro toxins

For humans and animals the greatest danger posed by fungi is the ability for some species to produce mycotoxins. Mycotoxins are the secondary metabolites of mould and fungi and are a chemical combination of organic acids and aromatic compounds. Investigations into the harmful capabilities of these toxins date back to the 1960's when aflatoxin was first found on peanuts, but no doubt the chronic and acute symptoms that mycotoxins cause in humans and animals have been experienced for many thousands of years.

At present there is still a vast amount of knowledge that is not known about fungi and their associated mycotoxins. Of the 300400 mycotoxins reconsigned only about a dozen receive regular attention for their potential threats to human and animal life (Paterson 2006).

For many years fungi have been used in products for human use. Penicillium was developed for medical purposes and the Koji mould is used widely in Japanese fermented foods like sake and miso. The safety of using these fungi have come into question as new strains are emerging that could potentially produce mycotoxins in established products.

Mould reservoirs and amplifiers There are two distinctly different indoor environments which harbour mould - mould reservoirs and mould amplifiers. A reservoir is where mould can be deposited and even accumulate, but will not necessarily multiply. Carpets are perhaps the best examples of mould reservoirs. A mould amplifier is an environment which enables the mould to grow. This can be any material with a relative humidity of more than 65%, with the ideal range being 85% - 90%. The mould will flourish and is able to develop and release its spores. Bathroom ceilings or wet carpet become mould amplifiers. The prime area is in poorly designed bathrooms where the ventilation is via a small window.

Some moulds produce toxins. These varieties, such as aspergillus, penicillium, stachybotrys and arimonium are water loving and their growth is harmful, but does not usually occur in concentrated amounts indoors. In order to grow, mould needs water, warmth and a food source. A leaky roof, burst pipe or other type of water penetration provides a moist area suitable for growth, especially if the area is never thoroughly dried out. Cellulose-based sheet rock, gypsum and other standard building materials provide a nutrient smorgasbord for mould. Many common building techniques can prevent moisture from drying up and incidentally promote mould growth. The problem is often exacerbated by tearing down a contaminated wall and enabling the mould and its spores to become airborne.

Some varieties, such as stachbotrys, are heavier than air and tend to settle on surfaces. If you take out a wall with stachybotrys, you have unwittingly distributed tens of thousands of spores and mould particles that will settle around the room. If a child sits on a chair and disturbs the particles, they become respirable. This is how contamination occurs, with possibly serious results.

Mould contamination occurs most frequently in grouting and behind silica beading. The staining from mould growth is obvious in these areas. Overflow from potplants may appear innocuous, but if an underlying surface such as carpet or matting becomes damp, mould will thrive. Stains can be removed, but if action is delayed, mould will permanently damage the carpet fibres.

Areas of major concern are those that have become water damaged from leaking pipes or rain. These areas are often overlooked until they start emitting unpleasant odours. By then the mould is already producing toxic chemicals - gasses and allergens in the form of tiny spores and particles. If you identify any mould or water damage, act quickly. It only takes a few days for a serious problem to develop, not only in terms of health, but also in terms of cost, as both your health and the contaminated materials deteriorate quickly.

Effects of mould on your health

Exposure to mould spores is more serious than previously thought. The effects of moulds and dampness on the respiratory health of children are comparable to the effects of passive smoking and can also cause asthma and chronic bronchitis. In a recent USA study of asthma in inner city suburbs, the mould Altenaria was found to be the single most important factor associated with the disease.

In damp and mouldy houses, people are more likely to suffer from rhinitis, nasal congestion, coughs, wheezing and sore throats. Mould exposure is associated with being more susceptible to colds, lower respiratory tract infections and irritation of skin and eyes, fever and headache. In severe cases exposure can cause death.

Mould is being called 'the asbestos of a new generation' in the United States and a rash of lawsuits totaling $US600 million is pending. A recent legal case resulted in the payout of $US3.1 million dollars by a company which did not adequately clean up a mould contaminated home.

Mould problems are not limited to homes. In Los Angeles, a condominium association is suing real estate developers, contractors and managers for personal injury and property damage. The cause? Inadequate waterproofing which permitted toxic mould to grow. A school and a city hall annexe in Cambridge Massachusetts shut down because of mould contamination. In Los Angeles, a Superior Court judge and court employees are suing the county for failing to repair a leaky air conditioner unit that caused a 'black, slimy mould' to colonise the courtroom resulting in severe rashes, respiratory problems, dizziness and abdominal pains. In an extreme case in Cincinnati, an aspergillus strain bred to plague proportions before detection, contaminating ventilation systems, bathrooms and behind walls. The general manager who conducted the clean-up developed pulmonary fibrosis, and with only half his lung capacity left, now takes a cocktail of 17 drugs each day to survive.

Around the world, mould is identified in up to one third of buildings. Even in dry climates, buildings may be closed up, allowing the humidity to rise and mould to flourish.

Closer to home, in Perth, Western Australia, a family became ill with respiratory complications, debilitating fatigue and candida when their bathroom became contaminated by mould. When the problem was remediated successfully, their chronic health problems disappeared over a period of a week.

A number of residents are now taking action against negligent landlords. In one case, a family was exposed for 18 months to mould on ceilings and most of their walls. All seven people in the home were ill with respiratory symptoms and all the children were asthmatic.

Peter has become involved in dozens of cases of mould contamination in buildings and receives several calls a week from building managers and private home owners seeking remedial measures.

Fixing the problem

Humidity is an important consideration when controlling mould, however, a more important factor is water content at the surface. Humid air condenses onto a surface as it becomes cooler, as when a steamy bathroom cools down. Materials like cement, wood and carpets then act as sponges and become a breeding ground for mould.

By keeping indoor surfaces clean and dry, and maintaining a relatively low humidity, that is, below 50%, growth can be prevented. Regular and thorough cleaning of appliances where micro-organisms can grow, fixing leaks, repairing tile grouting, thoroughly mopping up standing water and eradicating damp areas (which also helps to decrease humidity) will deprive mould of its growing conditions. Regular and quality maintenance of air conditioning equipment is also necessary.

Disinfectants, bleaches and phenols combat most contamination. However, these chemicals are themselves known to have adverse effects on human health. A low toxicity solution is advisable so that you do not inadvertently replace one problem with another.

Remedial action is easier if guidelines are followed. Check regularly for mould in wet areas, including air conditioning systems. Any amount on the walls and ceilings can be toxic and requires remedial action. If you can see mould anywhere, other than in the tile grouting (where it is almost impossible to eliminate) you have a problem. If there is an earthy, musty, or 'old sock' odour, you can assume you have a mould problem. You or someone else in your household may be experiencing symptoms such those previously listed. Look for previous water damage. Visible mould growth is found underneath materials where water has damaged the external surfaces, or it may be growing invisibly behind walls or in the roof. Look for discolouration and leaching from plaster. Don't go to the trouble and expense of testing as a first step in detection, as reliable sampling is expensive and requires equipment not available to the general public.

The major focus of any remediation is to first control the water or moisture at its source. Follow the water tract and eliminate it. Then remove the colonised materials or decontaminate the surface.

Cleaning small areas

Prepare a solution of vinegar with clove oil. Wear protective clothing, such as rubber gloves and a long-sleeved shirt. Apply the solution to the mouldy area gently with a sponge or mop –

spraying is not advised as it can cause spores to become airborne and spread to other locations. Allow the vinegar solution to stay in contact with the surface for 15 minutes or more. Ensure the treated area dries out as moulds will regrow if the surface remains damp. If the surface is solid (not flaking or absorbent), a simple solution of detergent can be used.

Ventilation systems should also be visually checked, particularly for damp filters, overall cleanliness and for damp conditions elsewhere in the system. Ceiling tiles, gypsum wallboard (sheet rock), cardboard, paper, and other cellulose surfaces should be given careful attention during a visual inspection. Stop any water seepage. To limit mould growth, you must respond to water damage within 24 to 48 hours with a thorough clean up, drying, and/or removal of water damaged materials.

If your home has large areas of mould, a professional contractor should be called as removal must be done by someone with specialist training. Tenants should immediately contact their landlord if mould appears in any part of the home. Deal with mould problems quickly. Acting swiftly with preventative measures will protect health and may avert litigation.

PART FIVE

Chapter 19. Radiation

Radiation is simply energy travelling through space. Radiation moves through space at the speed of light as waves of electric and magnetic energy. While maintaining the speed of light, these waves oscillate at various frequencies along a continuum called the "electromagnetic spectrum." At one end of the spectrum is high-frequency energy such as X-rays, cosmic rays and nuclear radiation, while at the other end of the spectrum is low-frequency energy such as AC power. Near the centre of the electromagnetic spectrum is visible light and infrared radiation; descending from these visible frequencies are microwaves and radio waves.

Non-ionising radiation includes the spectrum of ultraviolet (UV), visible light, infrared (IR), microwave (MW), radio frequency (RF) and extremely low frequency (ELF) radiation. An example of non-ionising radiation most familiar to us is sunshine. Non-ionising radiation differs from ionising radiation in that the wavelengths of the former are longer and the frequency of the waves is lower, hence the overall energy of the wave is lower.

By contrast, ionising radiation has sufficient energy to excite the electrons in the orbitals of an atom, causing them to become charged. Exposure to even low doses of ionising radiation - such as X-rays and radioactive materials including uranium and radon—can cause cancer and birth defects.

Chapter 20. Non-ionising Electromagnetic Radiation

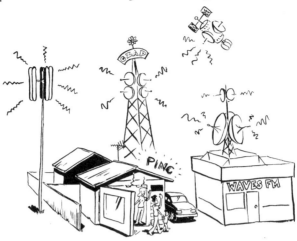

People may be exposed to non-ionising radiation through natural sources such as the sun as well as human-generated sources: computers, microwaves ovens, mobile phones, radar systems and power lines. From the sun, UV radiation is a major concern related to sunburn, skin damage and skin cancer. Too much sun can have a negative effect on one's immune system. On the other hand, without enough exposure to the sun, the body does not produce vitamin D.

Microwave radiation

Microwaves are extremely high frequency radio waves on the electromagnetic radiation spectrum. Though sometimes referred to generally as radiofrequency waves, microwaves specifically occupy the frequency range 300MHz to 300GHz.

While some microwaves and radiofrequency radiation occur naturally—the sun, the earth and the ionosphere create natural sources of low-level RF and MW radiation fields—the incidence of non-naturally occurring radiation has increased dramatically with the advance of technology. Microwaves can be used to carry satellite signals for communication in televisions, AM and FM radio, computers, global positioning systems and mobile phones. Microwaves can also be used to generate heat through the extremely rapid reversal in the polarity of electrons affected by magnetic and electric fields via a tube called a magnetron—this occurs in almost every kitchen and restaurant throughout the industrialised world, with the ubiquitous microwave oven.

Microwaves and radiofrequencies represent one of the most common and fastest growing environmental influences about which anxiety and speculation are spreading. Yet very little is known about the results of exposure to microwaves; even less is known about the relative dangers of different sources of microwaves. We do, however, know that microwaves can be reflected, transmitted or absorbed by matter in their path. Absorption occurs in matter that contains moisture, including human beings.

Living organisms absorb microwaves and radiofrequency energy at the molecular, cellular, tissue and whole-body levels. Heating of internal organs is a consequence of the absorption of energy. The energy is absorbed by water within the tissue; therefore, tissues with high water density and low blood density - such as the eyes and testes - are particularly vulnerable.

Scientists have known for a long time about the capacity of RF radiation to cause this type of heating and have discovered that prolonged exposure to RF radiation can lead to health problems such as fatigue, reduced mental concentration and, in the case of very high levels, cataracts. These effects are similar to subjecting a person to an extremely warm environment. Other possible thermal effects include foetal abnormalities, decreased thyroid function, cardiovascular mortality, impaired ability to perform complex tasks and the suppression of behavioural responses, gonadal function and natural killer cell activity. Studies have shown that environmental levels of microwaves and radiofrequency energy routinely encountered by the general public are far below levels necessary to produce significant heating and increased body temperature. However, there is concern for whole body heating amongst the elderly and those on specific medications that affect thermoregulatory function. Also of concern are people with cardiac and circulatory problems, those with implanted medical electronic devices (e.g., heart pacemakers), fever sufferers, infants and pregnant women.

The majority of studies in this area are concerned with cataracts, arguably the major hazard associated with microwave radiation. A cataract is a clouding of the lens within the eye. Authorities concerned with producing safety standards agree that little is known with any real certainty about the effects of microwave radiation beyond its thermal effects. However, microwave studies contain too many shortcomings to rule out the possibility that microwaves cause adverse health effects.

Non thermal effects

The recognition of non-thermal effects has been highly controversial, due to conflicting and inconclusive studies. Studies are complex, investigating possible effects of microwave radiation—from cancer to effects on the operation of all systems and parts of the human body. Cancer studies have examined cancers of the breasts, lungs, testicles and brain, as well as ocular melanoma and leukaemia. Other studies have included assessments of the relationships between radiation and cardiovascular disease, birth defects and hormone secretion rates. Research has also shown the effect of microwaves on reducing a cell's ability to perform apoptosis, increasing the risk for fixation and other spontaneous mutations, including cancer.

An example of the controversy surrounding microwaves occurred with a 1990 leaked draft EPA report in the USA, recommending that radiofrequency microwave radiation be considered a "possible human carcinogen." The White House moved quickly to suppress the draft and commissioned another report, which stated that there was no EMF cancer risk. Unfortunately, politics has its influence in too many places it should not.

The ever-increasing use of electrical appliances, along with the consequent demand for electric power, have greatly increased awareness of possible risks from electric and magnetic fields at extremely low frequencies. In particular, concern has been raised about power lines. This concern has, in some cases, led to strong opposition to the installation of transmission facilities, which has delayed or even prevented their licensing. The proximity to power lines in suburbs usually means less demand for the properties and lower real estate values due to concerns about raising families near these powerful sources of electro-magnetic radiation.

The idea that such fields might be deleterious has been seriously considered only since 1979, when researchers suggested, on the basis of a case-control study conducted in Colorado, that the fields associated with power lines and domestic electric wiring might cause cancer in children. At the time the idea seemed bizarre—power lines were such a normal part of everyday life and they had not been shown in laboratory experiments to have any effect that appeared to be even remotely connected with the development of cancer. During the past 25 years, however, numerous epidemiological studies have suggested a link between leukaemia and brain cancer in adults and exposure to similar and higher frequency fields at work. Residential-based studies have found similar links. The findings are, however, difficult to interpret. One reason for this is that neither leukaemia nor brain cancer is a single entity; each consists of a variety of conditions that differ in childhood and adult life and may—and in some cases definitely do—have complex causes.

Residential studies do not always directly measure exposure, but frequently use surrogates. These surrogates might include the distance of the residence from overhead power lines or electrical transmission stations or the wiring configurations in the vicinity of the residence, which could be classified as "high" or "low" according to the presence or absence of transformers and the characteristics of the local electricity supply cables. However, in three Scandinavian studies in 1993, children who lived in houses within broad corridors around power lines had higher than normal rates of leukaemia and brain cancer. Other studies have shown similar results: the incidence of leukaemia with residential exposure equal to or greater than 0.2 µT (or 0.25 µT in the Danish series) was 2.1 times that in the unexposed population. A recent study in Canada, in which participants wore personal monitoring devices, supports a link between magnetic field exposure and an increased risk of childhood leukaemia. Evidence of a carcinogenic effect in adults has been supported by studies that have suggested occupational hazards for leukaemia and cancer of the brain.

In a three-year study of some 570 people in Auckland, New Zealand researchers found that people living within 20 metres of high-tension power lines were three times as likely to have asthma, twice as likely to experience major depression, twice as likely to suffer from immune deficiencies (including allergies and dermatitis) and more likely to have diabetes than those who did not live within such proximity to power lines.

Researchers have also found significant evidence that

occupational exposure to electromagnetic fields may reduce melatonin levels. Melatonin levels appear to be affected by the intensity and length of exposure as well as time of day it occurred; levels did not return to normal when workers were away on weekends. Melatonin, produced by the body, regulates sleep cycles and is a potent antioxidant that protects us from cancer.

The magnetic field strength produced by overhead lines depends mainly on the current flowing and distance from the line. Unlike the voltage, the current may change considerably during the day according to the demand for energy and, therefore, the magnetic field from power lines will be highly variable, reaching its maximum values when the load is highest—that is, when many people are using electrical appliances.

In addition, the magnetic field depends on the height above ground and configuration of conductors as well as, in the case of double- or multiple-circuit lines, on the sequence of phases of each circuit. The level of electromagnetic radiation from the power lines at ground level may reach a maximum value of about 20 µT in correspondence to the axis of a single-circuit 380 kV line, while at a distance of 50 metres from the centre of the line it decreases to values of the order of 1 µT. Objects and buildings provide little or no screening for the magnetic field. In other words, even though it is safer to be farther from power lines, buildings don't block out the magnetic field.

Exposure to electromagnetic radiation from appliances in buildings is also an area of growing concern. The results from measurements in some offices show that magnetic induction levels are within the range 0.2 3.2 µT close to typical office devices such as personal computers and photocopiers, while at the writing desks and in usual conditions the mean value is equal to 0.37 µT, with a maximum value of 1.4 µT. Most new computers have a screening device on the front but unfortunately not behind the computers so don't sit behind a computer. In a few buildings we have investigated, wiring ran inside internal columns in the buildings, with people working right next to the columns. The exposure was extremely high and resulted in many health complaints. Devices to measure electromagnetic radiation are relatively cheap and can be obtained from some electrical stores.

In the home environment, the most significant exposure is likely to come from electrical equipment, clocks and lights in the bed head or near where people sleep. In addition, exposure can be considerable if the bed backs onto a wall that has a circuit board behind it. In general the bedroom should not have too many electrical devices in it and none near the area where one's head is during sleep.

Chapter 22. Mobile Phones

While there is significant controversy about the use of mobile phones and whether they will cause or contribute to particular diseases, there is no doubt that they have the potential to cause harm. A serious problem lies with our inability to measure the relationship between our exposure to radiofrequency radiation and resulting disease. Just as difficult is separating out the roles of vested interests. While the weight of evidence from industry and government studies suggests that there is little, if any, problem, the majority of evidence from independent studies indicates that there are very serious issues that require careful consideration. However, once technology is rolled out it is almost impossible to roll it back.

The problem with mobile phones is that they emit radio frequency from the base station antennas, producing low but continuous exposure to entire communities and to the mobile phone or handset, which produces intense, intermittent exposure to the head of the user. Mobile telephones operate on sending and receiving frequencies in the approximate range of 825 MHz to 915 MHz, although with the continued expansion of this technology, the range of frequencies to which users are potentially exposed may be broadened to 450 MHz to 2500 MHz. The antenna of the phone radiates power equally in all directions at peak levels of 1-2 W when the phone is operating. Also emitted from the phone is a low-frequency magnetic field, associated with surges in electric current from the battery, generally in the range of 0.125 W – 0.25 W.

The amount of this radiation that is actually absorbed by the user varies according to the amount of power emitted from particular phones. The amount of power depends on design factors such as make, model and type of aerial as well as individual use of the device—including the proximity of the phone to the ear or skull, the orientation of the phone and the use of "hands-free" phone kits. The proximity of the phone to the user's head has been found to have the most significant relationship between mobile phone use and the amount of microwave and radiofrequency radiation the head absorbs.

From the phone being in contact with the head, the amount of power that is absorbed decreases exponentially as the phone is moved farther away from the ear. The amount of power that is absorbed can decrease by as much as 25 percent with the phone being placed one centimetre from the head when in use. "Hands-free" kits are also a practicable means of reducing exposure to radiation by two orders of magnitude, due to the increased distance of the phone to the sensitive tissues of the human body. Similarly, the use of the speakerphone held away from the head can also dramatically reduce exposure.

Health effects

The effects of non-ionising radiation from mobile phones can be broadly categorised into thermally (heat) induced and non-thermally induced biological effects. Non thermal effects of mobile phones include headache, memory problems, increase in frequency of seizures in children, decrease in duration of deep sleep and inhibition of secretion of melatonin.

Typical effects that have been noted in human studies include radiofrequency sickness, electroencephalographic changes, cell proliferation, blood pressure changes and blood-brain barrier leakages. Also confirmed have been transient, but significant, modifications in dermal or cutaneous blood flow as a result of standard operation of mobile phones. There are many less severe effects linked to mobile phone use; these include headache, sore muscles (radiating from the ear to the temple and through the shoulders) and sleep disturbances.

There is also growing concern about the potential contribution of mobile phones to brain cancer, leukaemia and acoustic neuroma (a particular tumour) in the head and neck. Few epidemiological studies have managed to confirm a solid link between mobile phone usage and tumour formation; making such links is extremely complicated due to issues such as the latency period between exposure and onset of symptoms. It may also be due to the strong industry bias in research. However, several population and surrogate studies have produced alarming results. In a national US study, a significantly increased incidence of neuroepithelial tumours was found to be consistent with mobile phone usage. This was indicated by increased DNA strand breaks and chromosomal aberrations, which promote the development of tumours. Other studies have reported similar findings, noting changes in the development of enzymes associated with carcinogenesis after exposure to radiofrequency radiation. This suggests that the influence of radiofrequency and microwave radiation is more localised to the source of the energy and perhaps aided by the ability of radiofrequency radiation to interfere with the blood-brain barrier. This is supported in surrogate studies, which showed influences on immuno-reactivity and neurotransmitters within the brain.

The impact of radiofrequency on male reproductive organs is also an area of increasing distress due to the known interference of radiofrequency and microwave radiation on the testes. A recent study found that electromagnetic radiation from mobile phones interferes with human sperm motility, the ability of the sperm to progress through the reproductive tract. This is of prime concern as this interference may lead to structural and behavioural changes in the male germ cell that may not be apparent until later in life. In a study of laboratory animals exposed to low-energy radiofrequency radiation (that is, from a mobile phone), the exposure group experienced higher percentages of non-progressive or no-motility sperm. This could generate problems in the future for many, given the young age at which individuals start to use mobile phones.

While there are many concerns about the use of mobile phones, most governments are locked into the continued and expanded use of these devices. Authorities around the world are vague on the subject of mobile phones, mainly because of economic reasons. Despite this, the World Health Organization recommends that one limit time on mobile phones and use hands free devices whenever possible. The WHO also advises to use a "land line" phone when available, limit the duration of mobile phone conversations, fully extend the phone's antenna where possible (i.e., if the phone has an external antenna) and use one's mobile phone in an open area so the phone transmits at a lower power level.

The controversy about the health effects of mobile phones is illustrated by a 2001 report from the Independent Expert Group on Mobile Phones, which stated that children under the age of 16 should be discouraged from using these devices. The reason for this recommendation is the potential for children to absorb more energy from radiation as a result of their relatively smaller head sizes, thinner skulls and higher tissue conductivity. The age recommendation was lowered to 10 years in 2004. This was due to pressure from the mobile phone companies, especially given that teenagers are probably the biggest users of mobile phones and these companies could have lost a significant portion of a growing, captive market.

Mobile phone towers emit microwave signals in a relatively wide beam. These emissions have intensities that are quite high at close range to the antenna but which drop in intensity with distance. By any measure, the level of the signal is relatively low on the ground but residents nearby are exposed to these emissions 24 hours a day. No one knows the long-term effects of this type of exposure or the range of susceptibility.

Radon

In contrast to non-ionising radiation discussed in earlier chapters, ionising radiation releases large amounts of energy, which can significantly change atoms and molecules—including DNA. However, the only real concern in homes from ionising radiation is the naturally occurring radioactive gas radon, which is released during the decay of uranium-238 (U-238). Particulates in the indoor environment become radioactive when radon gas seeps into a building and decays into various radioactive elements, which attach to larger particles. The characteristics of these particles are similar to those of the radioactive elements themselves, thus posing the same health risks.

Before the 1930s, radon was not thought to have carcinogenic properties. However, we now know that persons breathing elevated concentrations of radon gas over time are at increased risk of lung cancer. According to the EPA, radon is the second-leading cause of lung cancer, "responsible for about 21,000 lung cancer deaths every year." Radon has been identified as the causal agent in five percent of lung cancer cases in the UK; the figures for Australia are estimated to be similar to those in the UK.

It is the process by which radon breaks down that led to it being labelled a carcinogen. The decay by-products of radon are themselves radioactive and release cancer-causing alpha particles, which are directly responsible for radon's carcinogenicity. When it comes in contact with a cell, radon's decay process causes it to emit alpha particles. The theory is that some of these particles, which can damage cell tissue, reach the nuclei of the cells. Mutation in the nuclei means that the genetic information of that cell is damaged and subsequent cell division can result in the proliferation of mutated cells and the formation of cancer. The evidence is very solid that radon causes lung cancer in animals.

While the inhalation of radon from the air can expose the epithelial cells of the lungs to alpha particles, the inert nature of radon has a more sinister influence on the rest of the body. Its inert nature means that radon can rapidly diffuse across the alveolar membrane of the lungs, where it can be absorbed into the blood. (Radon progeny, on the other hand, have great difficulty getting across this barrier due to their charged nature.) Once in the bloodstream, radon is transported to all parts of the body where, again through diffusion, it can be taken up by various organs. The accumulation of radon and its progeny in red bone marrow and possible results of this were first brought to the scientific world's attention in 1989, when scientists found a positive correlation between indoor radon concentration in homes and the occurrence of acute myeloid leukaemia (AML) in the UK. Though these findings have been vigorously debated, a wide array of evidence supports them.

Radon in indoor spaces may originate from emissions from rock, particularly igneous rock (formed from molten rock) and soils around the building or from construction materials used in walls, floors and ceilings. Many population centres are built upon earth rich in uranium. The Colorado area in the United States, because of predominance of igneous rock structures, is one example. This increased concentration of U-238 encourages higher levels of radon.

The entry of radon into a building is determined by the structural characteristics of, and the flow of radon-containing air into, the building. In most cases, radon gas enters buildings primarily through the under-structure, through a pressure differential created by the building itself. Radon can enter a building via any crack or other route which links subsurface soil to the inside of the building; these routes include water pipes, cracks in building joints, sump holes, crawl spaces and spaces surrounding electrical wiring.

A phenomenon known as the "stack effect" can also lead to high radon levels. This occurs mainly in winter, when the artificial heating of houses leads to a notable temperature difference from the outside environment and hence greater differences in relative air pressures. To promote efficiency, the upper parts of houses are usually insulated, thus the main place from which air is drawn into the house is the soil, which promotes greater uptake of radon. Various factors can increase or decrease the amount of radon taken up from the soil. Studies have linked topography, precipitation, summertime conditions and temperature in general to changes in concentrations of indoor radon from subsurface sources.

Building materials such as heavy stone and bricks made from industrial refuse (a popular practice in the 1970s) may also contain elevated levels of radon. Therefore, the type of material used for construction may lead to an increase in indoor radon concentrations, though the effect is relatively small and often debated. Another source thought to contribute to indoor radon levels, albeit small, is the use of natural gas in cooking and heating.

Water is a minor source of indoor radon but a source nonetheless.

Radon can enter the home through water in one of two ways. It may be present in the water as dissolved radon, which escapes into the air or it may come in via radium present in the water, which subsequently breaks down into radon. Radon gas in water can escape into the air through the use of the water, particularly if it is heated, sprayed or agitated. Underground water sources absorb large quantities of radon as the gas has no other avenue of escape. Charcoal filtration and outdoor aeration are methods used to lower the radon concentration in domestic water originating from aquifers and deep wells.

Concern over the risk of radon exposure is tepid within the general population. Radon is a colourless, odourless gas, the health effects of which often do not become apparent until after a 20- to 40-year latency period. The risks of indoor radon remain extremely controversial, even though radon is an established occupational carcinogen. If we accept that radon in large amounts can cause lung cancer, then the question remains as to whether radon can cause lung cancer at lower household levels. Those most likely to be exposed to household radon are women and young children who spend much of their time in the home environment.

In Australia, all precautionary actions are totally voluntary, with no legislation in place. The individual's own sense of perceived risk will determine whether he or she actively seeks to take precautionary measures against radon. The task of reducing radon levels can be attempted in one of two ways, though a combination of both is more likely to be effective. One can reduce the level of radon already present in the air or attempt to prevent the radon from entering the building in the first place. The latter approach is likely to be more effective as a single measure and more cost-effective in the long term. It addresses the main reason that radon levels and indoor air quality in general have become a problem in recent years: lack of ventilation in buildings, allowing build-up of hazardous pollutants.

An obvious, low-cost way to mitigate an indoor radon problem is to increase ventilation. This can be achieved by simply opening windows and doors. Apart from increasing the flow of fresh air, this also negates the effect of the pressure differential. Increased ventilation can also be achieved by ducting fresh air into the house and used air out of the house.

Everything possible should be done to ensure that radon entry routes into the home are minimised. This involves sealing all cracks and crevices in floor slabs, walls and joints. Wiring and water pipes must be given special attention as they can act like a ducting vent due to the pressure differential that they create.

Radon in Australia

Australian homes are considered to have radon levels similar to those found in the UK but lower than those in the US. The construction of basements in US homes increases the infiltration of radon into homes. This is not a common practice in Australia. However, homes built on, around or near large rock formations are much more likely to have higher radon levels and even radon levels of concern. Examples of this would be in the Blue Mountains of Sydney and in the hills of Perth. I have been in homes and monitored extremely high levels when a home is built into natural rock and the rock is used as an internal feature of the home. Other high levels I have monitored include those in homes in small valleys when there are cool winds that concentrate the radon downhill.

We do know enough that, going forward, we must insist that legislation monitor where new homes are built in order to protect people from deadly radon.

Chapter 24. Sick Building Syndrome

"Sick Building Syndrome" is one of those terms that we have all heard, but which most of us don't really understand. Sick Building Syndrome (SBS) can basically be defined as an illness associated with the indoor environment where the symptoms are nonspecific and the causes of the symptoms are unknown. This is coupled with the fact that the occupants often feel much better soon after leaving the building. If the cause of the disease is known, such as in the case of Legionnaires' disease, the term "Building Related Illness" is used.

Generally people suffering from SBS experience irritation of the eyes, nose, throat and lower airways, skin reactions, unspecific hypersensitivity reactions, mental fatigue, headache, nausea or dizziness whilst they are in the premises. Sick Building Syndrome is associated with buildings used for non-industrial purposes, especially office blocks, although it occurs elsewhere. In developed economies it has been estimated that 30 percent of new and remodelled office blocks show signs of SBS and that 10 to 30 percent of occupants are affected. The estimated costs of SBS to industry in Australia are certainly in the hundreds of millions of dollars per year.

Sick Building Syndrome is a growing concern for builders, building owners and managers because of the potential legal ramifications if the problem is not adequately addressed. For employers it is a problem because it is likely to lower worker efficiency and, to a lesser degree, increase absenteeism. It is obvious that if workers are unhappy and irritated they are unlikely to be working at maximum capacity. While some studies have failed to show that Sick Building Syndrome has adverse effects (on stress, memory, vigilance, reaction time and steadiness), others have estimated that a 20 percent reduction in efficiency may occur.

The evidence from surveys suggests that some people have a predisposition to SBS. Some of the factors that appear to predispose people to SBS are gender, with women reporting symptoms more frequently, life stress, job stress, job satisfaction, job position, lifestyle and some psychosocial factors.

A number of studies have identified building factors associated with the presence and prevalence of Sick Building Syndrome. These factors include wall-to-wall carpets and large areas of upholstery, shelves and horizontal surfaces. In the office, photocopying, handling carbonless copy paper and working with video display units have been shown to be related to SBS symptoms. Other factors that have been associated with SBS include crowding, office size and poor environmental control by individuals.

What is clear in almost all of the research is that people in buildings with all or some natural ventilation report fewer symptoms than those who work in buildings that use a ventilation system only. In addition, natural ventilation is healthier than water-based systems. In support of this, research has found that more than 50 percent of problems are due to poorly designed, operated or maintained heating, ventilation and air conditioning systems.

Causes of Sick Building Syndrome

Sick Building Syndrome is not a single disease; it is a syndrome resulting from a variety of factors. Some of these factors may be acting alone on the building occupants, while in most cases it is probably a combination of many factors working together. These include physical factors such as temperature, humidity, ventilation and airflow; chemical factors such formaldehyde and volatile organic compounds; biological factors such as mould, fungi, bacteria and dust mites; and psychosocial factors as mentioned above. Again these factors may work together to produce a sick building.

Physical factors can contribute to Sick Building Syndrome. Many investigations have highlighted factors such as climate (temperature and humidity), light intensity and flicker and irritating noises, such as low-frequency hum and resonance from air conditioning and rattles from faulty vents. Central heating boilers and pumps as well as lift mechanisms and forced air heating and cooling are the most common sources of unwelcome noise.

The type of air conditioning system and how it is placed within the structure of the building have been widely recognised as the major factors in Sick Building Syndrome. If the system malfunctions or is not kept clean and dry, SBS is often the result. Fluctuations in air velocity, leading to people finding the workplace "too draughty" or "too stuffy," are indicators that air distribution is unsatisfactory, even if the average air velocity is fine.

Some research has indicated that Sick Building Syndrome symptoms arise if the temperature goes below or above 21 to 22 degrees Celsius but this is just an average optimum temperature for people; temperature preference varies by individual. The optimum range of relative humidity (RH) is 45 to 55 percent, which is much narrower than previously thought. A wider range is acceptable for thermal comfort but encourages bacterial and fungal growth.

Research has shown that people can suffer, to varying degrees, a syndrome known as Seasonal Affective Disorder (SAD), which is a result of deprivation from full-spectrum lighting. It can result in lethargy, loss of interest in work and social activity as well as other symptoms. Many people intensely dislike working under fluorescent lights (which do not provide the full spectrum of light) and this will no doubt add to job stress. Many people prefer to have some control of their lighting and local environment but most offices are not designed for individuals to be able to adjust their own lighting.

Recent research has found strong associations between airborne dust and symptoms of Sick Building Syndrome. Some of our research identified inadequate cleaning equipment and some poor cleaning practices as contributing to elevated levels of dust in the air and an increase in SBS symptoms. By improving cleaning equipment and practices it was possible to reduce the number of symptoms and to provide a cleaner building.

With increasing media attention, it has been suggested that incidents of Sick Building Syndrome may occur that are caused by psychosocial rather than physical, chemical or biological agents. There is no research to suggest that Sick Building Syndrome is psychosocial in origin. However, research suggests that a psychosocial aspect may become a factor if occupant complaints are not adequately addressed.

Chemical factors include emissions of formaldehyde and other volatile organic compounds from new materials introduced into office buildings as well as activities such as cleaning. These are the same problems we identified in home environments.

Landmark lawsuits in the USA have recognised that it is the employer's responsibility to provide clean, safe air for employees. In Australia some cases are already before the courts. But education, rather than litigation, is the path to follow. If people understand the main causative factors of Sick Building Syndrome and are given the means of monitoring, controlling and alleviating these factors, top-down action on management will not be necessary.

Aside from education, perhaps the two most effective means of reducing the incidence of indoor air quality problems are design and maintenance. Designs that give consideration to indoor air quality will help avoid problems related to SBS.

Satisfactory indoor climate is of vital importance for health, comfort, work and productivity. Making indoor climate a priority makes economic sense. Ensuring that people are safe at work is the first, but not the only, goal.

CONCLUSION

Chapter 25. Controlling Indoor Air Pollution

Three core ways to control indoor air pollution are:

1. Eliminating or decreasing emissions at their source;

2. Improving ventilation; and

3. Filtering the air.

Perhaps the most effective and sensible method of controlling indoor air pollution is to eliminate or decrease the problem at the source. This is the main control method used by government and health agencies. It is relatively less expensive to control pollution at its source than to remove it once it is present. Although source control is effective, the use of ventilation and, if possible, filtration systems provides an even better quality indoor environment.

The three methods of controlling the source are:

1. Product substitution. Using building materials with low or negligible emissions instead of using pressed wood products;
2. Chemical substitution. Using eco-friendly paints, sealants, cleaning products and cosmetics, rather than those which emit harmful chemicals; and
3. Insulating products to reduce emissions. For instance, laminating particleboard on all surfaces will greatly reduce the emission of formaldehyde.

Ventilation is an important means of reducing indoor air pollutants. It also improves our psychological wellbeing. Ventilation has several advantages. It replenishes stagnant air with its burden of carbon dioxide, it dilutes body odours, environmental tobacco smoke and other odours and removes harmful gases and airborne particles. The simplest way to ventilate is by opening doors and windows. However, ventilation is not always possible due to poor outdoor air or temperature extremes.

Air filtration is also a viable option for many situations. The advantage of good air filtration is that it can take out virtually all the contaminants—chemical, biological and physical. In an office building study we conducted some yeas ago we had fewer health complaints in the offices where air cleaners had been installed. In another study we conducted in the homes of 60 asthmatic children, we found that a combination of air filtration and efficient vacuuming proved to be the most effective method of keeping the air clean. The vacuum reduced the larger micro-particles (10 microns) while the air filters removed more of the smaller micro-particles (2.5 microns and less). This study revealed that cleaner air provided an extra benefit—a number of people reported that their partner stopped snoring! One explanation for this is that with fewer allergens and irritants in the air, there was less inflammation of the mucous membranes and less restriction of air passages.

The five different parts a filter should include are: pre-filter, HEPA filter, activated carbon filter, catalytic sterilising layer and a negative ion generator. The only one on the market that meets my criteria and is still affordable is the Mountain Breeze by Russell Hobbs, which is why I have put my name to it. You can see the Mountain Breeze and me by visiting www.mountainbreeze.com.au.

The pre-filter is used to capture the big bits of particles in the air—everything from five or six hundred micro-metres (0.6 mm) to 100 (0.1 mm) or so microns. These are the little pieces of dust you can see when light comes through the window. It also catches the long fibrous materials from furniture and carpets. While this size particles are not a major health problem they can be annoying and be a trigger for sneezing.

The HEPA filter is made of extremely thin glass fibres pressed onto a pleated paper and is piggybacked with a pre-filter for removal of larger particles, thereby preventing the filter from becoming clogged. The HEPA filter is able to remove 99.97% of particles down to 0.3 micron in size. These are the really small particles that can get into your respiratory system and cause harm, the ones you want to clean out of the air. HEPA filters are so efficient and reliable that dust sensitive industries such as electronic chip manufacturing and satellite assembly use such filters.

Activated carbon filters remove chemicals by absorption. These are ideal for chemicals such as formaldehyde and VOCs and for odours from tobacco smoke to a rotten fish smell. The carbon in the filter needs to be replaced when it is saturated and can no longer absorb contaminants. Once it starts to smell, it is time to replace it.

Negative ion generators clean the air by sending out negative ions, which attach to microscopic particles. These charged particles then collide with each other and stick to various surfaces, removing them from the air. However, they still remain within the room, on the wall, carpet or any other surface to which they were attracted; this is why they are best used in conjunction with other filters. Negative ion generators affect only particles and do not remove volatile gases from the air. Various studies have shown that negative ions can have positive effects on our health and our sense of wellbeing. Naturally you find high levels of negative ions near waterfalls, beaches and in nature while you find very low levels in urban settings and homes and extremely low levels in polluted environments.

UV light is very effective against bacteria and viruses and is the last safeguard in a good filter system. However, UV light on its own requires the air to be exposed to the UV light for a long time. Recently Mountain Breeze has combined UV light technology with titanium dioxide to make the most effective organic catalytic system. It literally burns away the DNA. Considerable research is being conducted on its use in controlling TB in hospitals and in other high-risk environments.

A number of other factors need to be considered in the selection of a filter. They are:
- Efficiency: the ability of the filter to remove from the air stream the greatest number or percentage of particles;
- Pressure drop: the higher the resistance to the airflow due to the filter, the greater the amount of energy will be required to overcome it;
- Atmospheric dust holding capacity: the larger the amount of dust the filter can capture and hold, the less frequently the filter needs to be changed or serviced; and
- Capacity: the amount of air per unit time that the

filter can handle; this can affect its performance, such as its dust holding capacity.

With all this in mind you can understand why I recommend only the Mountain Breeze.

Other methods

"Bake-out" is a way of removing VOCs from building materials and furnishings and from motor vehicles. Although not a practical solution for most homes, it is an efficient way of removing VOCs from vehicles. Different chemicals off-gas at varying temperatures and one can achieve a good result by manipulating the temperature inside the vehicle. By closing up completely or allowing only limited ventilation through a small gap in the windows, the off-gassing of higher temperature VOCs will result. A high temperature off-gas should be followed by a period of maximum ventilation. Open all doors windows and sunroofs. This process should be continued daily until the "new car smell" is virtually negligible.

Plants as pollution control

A great deal of attention has been given to the use of plants to purify indoor air. One major experiment showed that certain plants are more efficient than others at removing different chemicals from the air. The effectiveness of plants as air purifiers has come under considerable critique as a result of the design of the experiments. The original studies, which showed plants as purifiers, were based on a single release of formaldehyde in sealed chambers. The major contributors to indoor formaldehyde concentrations are from composite woods, which continue to release formaldehyde over many years. The small scale of these experiments also made it difficult to extrapolate findings to real life situations.

Our study of plants and indoor air showed no change in formaldehyde concentrations with the addition of five or 10 plants in a small room and only an 11 percent reduction in formaldehyde concentrations with 20 plants in the room. This equalled more than two and a half plants per square meter of office space for just an 11 percent reduction. Opening a window 1 centimetre will achieve about the same or better reduction in formaldehyde and you will still have room to work. Plants are great for our sense of wellbeing and aesthetics but not for cleaning the air.

Chapter 26. To Finish

Every so often, a much-needed change comes along and the old way of doing things is thrown out like an old duster. The time has come to overhaul the way we think about our homes and other indoor environments because the problem of exposure to toxic chemicals is more serious than most people realized. This comes as a result of building materials, furnishings and activities such as cleaning continually releasing chemicals into the air we breathe. The exposure is long term and does not decrease over time (unless the only VOCs present are because the house is new). The home is where we find susceptible sectors of the population—the elderly, the very young and the infirm. Responsibility for reducing our exposure rests with us. It is impossible to avoid indoor air pollutants completely but we can minimise our exposure.

We need to rethink our cleaning practices and to clean using scientific principles. Cleaning for health rather than for cosmetics means reducing and controlling indoor dust. Awareness about the hazards of dust and biological contaminants means we also know just what it is we are cleaning and why. We need to invest in our health by buying vacuums that comply with the suction and filtration standards required for healthy cleaning. We need to stop using poor quality dusters and mops that resuspend dust and we need to apply cleaning and maintenance strategies that stop the growth of microorganisms and moulds.

We must cut down on the amounts of cleaning chemicals we use or replace them with safer alternatives, such as the simple products our grandparents used or microfibre technology, which cleans hygienically and does not require cleaning agents.

Healthy cleaning based on good science goes hand in hand with aesthetic, cosmetic cleaning. This is also a conscientious cleaning. Not only does it protect us, it also cares for and protects the earth, our home. This way we are cleaning not just for our future, but for the future of all who come after us to live on this beautiful blue planet.

Electromagnetic radiation is probably the most recent of the toxic exposures in our homes and all our buildings. While we are exposed to non-ionising radiation through natural sources such as the sun it is all the new human-generated sources—computers, microwaves ovens, mobile phones, radar systems and power lines—to which we continue to expose ourselves but about which we understand very little. The ever-increasing use of electrical appliances, including mobile phones and other hand held devices, and resulting increased demand for electric power, have greatly increased the possible risks to our health and to our planet.

While it is difficult to live without electrical devices, as with the issues of chemicals and dust there are small things everyone can do to make big differences in exposure. First you have to be aware of the problem, then willing to take action. Now take action!

I wish you and your family good health.

Scientific Publications by Dr Dingle on sick homes

1. Dingle. P and Hood, G. 1991. *Pollution Control and Public Health: Vehicle Emissions.* Presented at the Australian Institute of Environmental Health. Queensland Division. 51st State Conference. September 13-18 1991. Brisbane.

2. Dingle, P and Olden, P. 1992. *A Temporary Sick Building.* Australian Institute of Air Conditioning, Refrigeration and Heating. 30 April-1 May 1992. Perth Western Australia.

3. Dingle, P. and F. Murray 1992. *Air Quality in Indoor Environments.* Fourth Regional IUAPPA Conference, Air Quality for Sustainable Development. 5-12 July Brisbane.

4. Dingle, P and F. Murray 1992. *Control and regulation of indoor air: An Australian perspective. Quality Standards for the Indoor Environment: Scientific and Regulatory Aspects.* Prague, Czechoslovakia. 1-3 December.

5. Dingle, P, S Hu and F. Murray 1992. *Formaldehyde in a country with a Mediterranean climate. Quality Standards for the Indoor Environment: Scientific and Regulatory Aspects.* Prague, Czechoslovakia. 1-3 December.

6. Dingle, P 1992   *Sick or healthy buildings.* Occupational Health Society of Australia. Fourth Inaugural Conference. 11-13 November. Perth

7. Dingle, P 1993   Protocol for investigating buildings with occupant complaints. AIRAH International Conference April 5-7. Sydney.

8. Dingle, P and S. Hu 1993. *Formaldehyde in office buildings and the effect of plants on reducing formaldehyde.* AIRAH International Conference April 5-7. Sydney.

9. Dingle, P, P. Olden, S. Hu and F. Murray 1993. *A study of formaldehyde in an office building.* Indoor Air '93. The Sixth International Conference on Indoor Air Quality and Climate. July 4-8. Helsinki, Finland.

10. Dingle, P, S. Hu and F. Murray 1993. *Personal exposure to formaldehyde.* Indoor Air '93. The Sixth International Conference on Indoor Air Quality and Climate. July 4-8. Helsinki, Finland.

11. Gilbert, D, P. Dingle and K. Bentley 1993. *A National strategy for internal environmental health.* Indoor Air '93. The Sixth International Conference on Indoor Air Quality and Climate.

July 4-8. Helsinki, Finland.

12.   Hood, G and P. Dingle. 1993   *Poison on wheels.* Environment, Vol 14,3 pp 6-12

13.   Dingle, P.1993   *Healthy Buildings: An Australian Perspective.* Invited paper for CIB W77 Working Group on Health Buildings. July 8-9 Helsinki, Finland.

14.   Dingle, P 1993   *Formaldehyde and VOCs in Australian homes.* Invited speaker. Australian Institute for Environmental Health Annual Conference, Perth September 1-3.

15.   Dingle, P and P. Kemp 1994   *Indoor air pollution, productivity and symptoms in a new building.* AIRAH International Conference April. Brisbane

16.   Dingle, P , D. Williams and N. Runciman 1994   *Pesticides in homes: solution or problem.* Healthy Buildings '94. CIB-ISIAQ-HAS Conference Budapest, Hungary 22-25 August

17.   Dingle, P and A Stratico 1994   *Indoor air quality, risk communication and education Healthy Buildings '94.* CIB-ISIAQ-HAS Conference Budapest, Hungary 22-25 August

18.   Corbyn A.J and P. Dingle 1994   *Accumulation of exhaled air at the face of sleeping infants and sudden infant death syndrome.* Healthy Buildings '94. CIB-ISIAQ-HAS Conference Budapest, Hungary 22-25 August

19.   Kemp. P and P. Dingle. 1994   *Productivity and indoor air quality in a sick, new office building: a social and scientific problem.* Healthy Buildings '94. CIB-ISIAQ-HAS Conference Budapest, Hungary 22-25 August (submitted and accepted)

20.   Dingle, P. 1994   *Making Healthy Buildings.* Invited paper for CIB W77 Working Group on Health Buildings. Budapest, Hungary 25-26 August.

21.   Dingle, P. and B. Smith. 1994. *Indoor air pollution, exposure and health effects.* Proceedings of the12 The International Conference. Clean Air. 94. The Clean Air Society of Australia and New Zealand. Perth. Vol 1. p557-568. 23-28 October.

22.   Stratico. A and P. Dingle 1994   *Risk, Management, Perceptions and Air Pollution.* Clean Air. 94. 12 th International Conference. The Clean Air Society of Australia and New Zealand. Perth (submitted and accepted).

23.   Pontin. R, P Dingle and J Charlick. 1994. *Carbon monoxide in office buildings.* Clean Air. 94. 12 the International Conference.

The Clean Air Society of Australia and New Zealand. Perth.

24. Kemp. P and P. Dingle. 1994. The indoor environment, occupant symptoms and perceptions on a sick new office building. Clean Air. 94. 12 the International Conference. The Clean Air Society of Australia and New Zealand. Perth.

25. Dingle. P, S. Hu and F. Murray. 1994.   Personal Exposure To Indoor Air Pollutants. Indoor Air an Integrated Approach, International Workshop. Gold Coast Australia.

26. Dingle, P.1994.   Formaldehyde Exposure In Homes. Indoor Air An Integrated Approach, International Workshop. Gold Coast Australia.

27. Dingle, P, D. Williams and N. Runciman 1994. Pesticide, Policy and Problems. Indoor Air: An Integrated Approach, International Workshop. Gold Coast Australia.

28. Corbyn A.J and P. Dingle 1994   Carbon Dioxide Accumulation: A Factor In Sudden Infant Death Syndrome? Indoor Air an Integrated Approach, International Workshop. Gold Coast Australia.

29. Stratico. A and P. Dingle 1994.   Risk Perception and Indoor Air Quality. Indoor Air An Integrated Approach, International Workshop. Gold Coast Australia.

30. Bannister. M and P. Dingle. 1994. Monitoring Environmental Tobacco Smoke. Indoor Air An Integrated Approach, International Workshop. Gold Coast Australia.

31. Young. L, C. Barton and P. Dingle. 1994 The legal implications of Sick Building Syndrome. Indoor Air An Integrated Approach, International Workshop. Gold Coast Australia.

32. Kemp. P and P. Dingle. 1994. Dust Unkempt. Indoor Air An Integrated Approach, International Workshop. Gold Coast Australia

33. Kemp. P and P. Dingle. 1994. Productivity loss in a sick, new office building. Indoor Air An Integrated Approach, International Workshop. Gold Coast Australia.

34. Jiang. X, P Dingle and F Murray. 1994. Studies of indoor levels of nitrogen dioxide and formaldehyde in Perth. Waste treatment and resources. Xiaoming Zheng and Lizhong Zhu. Proceeding of the second Asian Symposium on Academic Activity for Waste treatment. pp 262-270.

35. Dingle. P. 1995. Indoor Air Quality in Australian Buildings. Australian Institute For Environmental Health. National

Conference. Perth.

36.   Kemp. P, P. Dingle. and J. Chalick. 1996. Seasonal variation in viable airborne bacteria concentrations in one building over three years. Indoor Air '96. The 7th International Conference on Indoor Air Quality and Climate. Vol 2. pp 1077-1082. July 21-26, 1996 Nagoya, Japan.

37.   Kemp. P and P. Dingle. 1996. Particulate matter in office buildings. Indoor Air '96. The 7th International Conference on Indoor Air Quality and Climate. Vol 1. pp 571-574. July 21-26, 1996 Nagoya, Japan.

38.   Stratico. A and P. Dingle 1996. Background fine particulate levels in Australian homes. Indoor Air '96. The 7th International Conference on Indoor Air Quality and Climate. Vol 1. pp 591-594. July 21-26, 1996 Nagoya, Japan.

39.   Dingle. P. and P Tapsell. 1996. Pesticide contamination resulting from the overuse of pesticides in Perth (Australia) homes. Indoor Air '96. The 7th International Conference on Indoor Air Quality and Climate. Vol 1. pp 595-598. July 21-26, 1996 Nagoya, Japan.

40.   Dingle. P. and S. Whyte. 1996. Contaminants in carpets in homes. Indoor Air '96. The 7th International Conference on Indoor Air Quality and Climate. Vol 1. pp 575-579. July 21-26, 1996 Nagoya, Japan.

41.   Franklin. P and P. Dingle. 1996. House dust mites in Perth homes. Indoor Air '96. The 7th International Conference on Indoor Air Quality and Climate. Vol 1. pp 671-676. July 21-26, 1996 Nagoya, Japan.

42.   Tapsell. P, P. Dingle. and A. Stratico. 1996. Healthy communication for healthy buildings: A study of risk communication in office buildings. Invited paper for CIB W77 Working Group on Healthy Buildings. July 20-21, 1996 Nagoya, Japan

43.   Dingle. P, P Tapsell and T Brown. Risk communication as a factor in Sick building Syndrome

44.   Whyte S.K. and P. Dingle 1996. Nutritional and Environmental Factors Affecting Asthma. Oceania Symposium of Complimentary Medicine. Queensland.

45.   Dingle. P, and A Stratico. 1997 Risk communication in Western Australia: Perceptions and information sources.

46.   Stratico A, Dingle P and P Franklin 1997 Risk communication

and indoor air quality. October 2-3 1997

47. Dingle. P and D. Farrar. 1998. Personal Exposure to Nitrogen Dioxide in buses, taxis and by bicycles in Perth. Clean Air Conference. October 19. Melbourne

48. Dingle. P. 1998. Environmental Challenges of the New Millennium. Annual State Conference of the Institute of Municipal Management. Oct 27-30. Perth Western Australia.

49. Franklin.P, P Dingle and S Stick 2000. Raised Exhaled Nitric Oxide in Healthy Children Is Associated with Domestic Formaldehyde Levels. Healthy Buildings 2000. August 6-10. Helsinki, Finland. Vol 1, 65- 70.

50. Farrar. D P. Dingle and P Franklin. 2000. Peak and long term Nitrogen Dioxide concentrations in Perth homes. Healthy Buildings 2000. August 6-10. Helsinki, Finland. Vol 1, 443-448

51. Na. G, P. Dingle and R. Tan 2000. Personal Exposure to Fine Particulates (PM2.5) in Homes Healthy Buildings 2000. August 6-10. Helsinki, Finland. Vol 1, 525-530

52. Na. G, P. Dingle and R. Tan 2000. Vacuum cleaners, the cause and the solution to indoor particulate matter. Clean Air and Environment conference 26-30 November. Sydney Australia.

53. Farrar. D P. Dingle and P Franklin. 2000. Nitrogen Dioxide concentrations and seasonal variations measured in urban homes in Western Australia. Perth. Clean Air and Environment conference 26-30 November. Sydney Australia

54. Dingle P 2001. Indoor air pollution, exposure and health effects. Environmental Health Odessey. 28th National Environmental Health Conference October 14-19. Perth Western Australia.

55. Dingle P 2001. Changing Directions: Cleaning for Health and the Environment. April Philladelphia USA

56. Cheong Cerdic Cheong Peter Dingle. variant indoor fungal levels in residential environments following a cleaning intervention on carpets & soft furnishings" for the IAQ 2002 conference.

57. White k and P Dingle. 2002 The effect of intensive vacuuming on indoor PM mass p92-97 Vol 3 . Proceedings of the 9th International Conference on Indoor Air Quality and Climate. Monterey California, June 30 –July 5.

58. Dingle P. R Tan and A Maynard 2002 Health effects, attitudes and perceptions toward cleaning. p8-103.Vol 3. Proceedings of

the 9th International Conference on Indoor Air Quality and Climate. Monterey California, June 30 –July 5.

59. Nastov J, R Tan P Dingle 2002 The study of hard floor surface cleaning practices and the effects on dust particulate in 8 Perth homes. P120-125 Vol 3. Proceedings of the 9th International Conference on Indoor Air Quality and Climate. Monterey California, June 30 –July 5.

60. White. K s Smith P Dingle 2002 HEPA air filtration:an effective method of reducing household PM exposure . p891-895 Vol 1 Proceedings of the 9th International Conference on Indoor Air Quality and Climate. Monterey California, June 30 –July 5.

61. Cheong C. H Neurimister -Kemp P Dingle J Hardy. 2002 Variant indoor fungal levels in residential environmental following a cleaning intervention and soft furnishings. P 1015-1020. Vol 1. Proceedings of the 9th International Conference on Indoor Air Quality and Climate. Monterey California, June 30 –July 5.

62. Cedric Cheong, Heike Neumeister-Kemp, Peter Dingle, Peter Kemp, Steve, Wilkinson, Nigel Wand Steve Brown 2008. Is your house killing you? Raising awareness of IAQ problems in homes in Australia. The 11th International Conference on Indoor Air Quality and Climate. Copenhagen Denmark, August 17-22.

63. Dingle. P 1997. Sick Building Syndrome. Cheremisinoff, P.N. Editor Health and Toxicology. Advances in Environmental Control and Technology Series. p 67-92. Gulf Publishing.

64. Dingle. P 1997. Pesticide Residues in Food. Cheremisinoff, P.N. Editor Health and Toxicology. Advances in Environmental Control and Technology Series. p 433-452. Gulf Publishing.

65. Dingle, P and F. Murray 1993. Indoor air: An Australian perspective. Indoor Environment Vol 2, 4, pp 217-220

66. Whyte. K and P Dingle 1997. Common Airborne Pollutants. Journal of the Australasian College of Nutritional and Environmental Medicine. Vol. 16. No 1. December. pp 5-17.

67. Kemp. P and P. Dingle. 1998. Particulate matter intervention Study: A Causal Factor of SBS in an older Building. Indoor Air. Vol 3: 153-171.

68. Dingle, P, D. Williams, N. Runciman, and P. Tapsell.

1999. Pesticides in Western Australian Homes. Bulletin of Environmental Contamination and Toxicology. Vol 62, 3.p309-314.

69. Dingle, P. and P Tapsell 1999.Exposure of Cabinet Makers to Formaldehyde Vapours. Australian and New Zealand Journal of Occupational Health and Safety. Vol 15, 3. June

70. Franklin.P, P Dingle and S Stick 1999. Formaldehyde Exposure in homes Associated with increased levels of nitric oxide in healthy children. Respirology. Vol 4 Supplement January.P A6

71. Franklin.P, P Dingle and S Stick 2000. Raised Exhaled Nitric Oxide in Healthy Children Is Associated with Domestic Formaldehyde Levels. American Journal of Respiratory and Critical Care Medicine. Vol 161: 1757-1759.

72. Dingle. P. P, Tapsell and S Hu. 2000. Reducing Formaldehyde Exposure in Office Environments Using Plants. Bulletin of Environmental Contamination and Toxicology. Vol 64: 302-308.

73. Heike G. Neumeister-Kemp, Cedric Cheong, Peter Kemp, Giles Hardy and Peter Dingle (2000). Indoor air fungi investigation of carpeted houses treated with different cleaning methods. Mycoses, Vol 43 No. 6, 247, Berlin Germany

74. Neumeister-Kemp, C.D. Cheong, P. C. Kemp, P. Dingle and G.E.StJ Hardy (2001) Alteration in indoor fungal levels via portable HEPA air filters in bedrooms of asthmatic children, Mycoses, Vol 44 No. 6, 244, Berlin Germany

75. Dingle. P, R Tan and C Cheong. 2000 Formaldehyde in occupied and unoccupied caravans in Australia. . Indoor and Built Environment. Indoor and Built Environment. 9.3-4. 233-236

76. Dingle. P, D Farrar and R Tan 2001. Exposure to nitrogen dioxide by buses, taxis and by bicycles in Perth, Australia. Bulletin of Environmental Contamination and Toxicology. Vol 66, 4. 433-438.

77. Dingle. P, R Tan and C Cheong. 2002 Personal exposure to formaldehyde in laboratories. Australian and New Zealand Journal of Occupational Health and Safety. Vol 18, (2) 161-166

78. Dingle P, R. Pontin and C Watkins.2002 Carbon monoxide in Perth office buildings. Australian and New Zealand Journal of Occupational Health and Safety. August Vol 18(4) 367-373.

79. Dingle. P, and R Tan. 2002. Formaldehyde in Retail Stores.

Australian and New Zealand Journal of Occupational Health and Safety. June Vol 18(3) 269-272.

80. Dingle. P and P Franklin. 2002. Formaldehyde Levels and the Factors Affecting These levels in Homes in Perth, Western Australia. Indoor and Built Environment. 11, 111-116.

81. Dingle P, P. Tapsell, and R Tan. (2002). Levels of Environmental Tobacco Smoke in 20 Social venues in Perth Western Australia. Indoor and Built Environment. Indoor and Built Environment 11, 146-152.

82. Dingle. P, F Lalla (2002) Indoor Air health Risk Perceptions in Australia. Indoor and Built Environment. Indoor and Built Environment. 11, 275-284.

83. Bannister. M, P Dingle, F Lalla (2003) Environmental Tobacco Smoke in Perth homes. Australian and New Zealand Journal of Occupational Health and Safety. August Vol 19(3)

84. Dingle. P.(2003) Formaldehyde concentrations and behaviour in office buildings Australian and New Zealand Journal of Occupational Health and Safety. August Vol 19(3)

85. Lalla. F and P Dingle (2004). The Antibacterial Action of Cloths and Sanitizers and the use of Environmental Alternatives in Food Industries . Journal of Environmental Health.

86. Cheong, C.D., Neumeister-Kemp, H.G., Dingle, P.W. and Hardy, G. St J. (2004) Intervention study of airborne fungal spora in homes with portable HEPA filtration units. J. Environ. Monit., DOI:10.1039/B408135H.

87. Cheong, C.D., Neumeister-Kemp, H.G., Dingle, P.W. and Hardy, G. St J. (2004) Cleaning intervention study: Reducing airborne indoor fungi and fine particulates in carpeted Australian homes using intensive, high efficiency HEPA vacuuming. J. Environ. Health Res. (submitted)

88. Cheong, C.D., Neumeister-Kemp, H.G., Dingle, P.W. and Hardy, G. St J. (2004) The Impact of Steam Cleaned Carpets on Airborne Fungal Spora and Fine Particulates in Residential Homes in Western Australia. Indoor Built Environ.

89. Farrar D, Dingle P, Runnion C and Franklin P. The effect of unflued gas heaters on residential nitrogen dioxide concentrations in Perth, Western Australia. Clean Air and Environmental Quality Journal 2005; 39: 46 50.

90. Peter Franklin, Tina Runnion, Drew Farrar and Peter Dingle.

(2007) Comparison of Peak and Average Nitrogen Dioxide Concentrations inside homes Atmospheric Environment

91.   Jones J, Stephen Stick, Peter Dingle and Peter Franklin Spatial variability of particulates in homes: implications for infant exposure. Atmos Env 2007.

Who is Dr Dingle

Dr D has a Bachelor of Education in Science, Bachelor of Environmental Science with first class honours, and a PhD. He is an Associate Professor in Health and the Environment at Murdoch University and one of Australia's best motivational health speakers. He has spent the past twenty years as a researcher, educator, communicator and author. He has more than 100 scientific papers, and 6 books.

Dr D has appeared on the Media for the last 20 years as expert in environmental and health issues and recently presented in the award winning 7 week TV series shown on SBS and now around the world "Is your house killing you". He is currently in the planning stages for another TV series. He is a regular on current affairs programs such as Today Tonight and ABC programs like "Can we help" and featured on 4 corners and the 7.30 report. He has appeared on occasions on Sunise, George Negus and other programs. He is a regular on Australian and New Zealand (TV3) TV and radio news and can be heard on a radio interview almost every day. He is reported weekly in the national media and writes a column for the west Australian and a number of public magazines.

Dr D commits to over a hundred public presentations each year. He is popular internationally for his lively presentations and has presented in 11 countries on 4 continents.

Dr D is a fully accredited member of the Australian Speaker's Association and a member of the Western Australian Society of Magicians. In his spare time he practices what he preaches, rides a bicycle to work, loves his wife Martine and family, the beach and the gym, juggles, plays with a unicycle and cooks a mean minestra (but not all at the same time!).

For further information and free downloads visit

www.drdingle.com

Other Books by Dr D.

The Deal for Happier, Healthier, Smarter Kids. A Twenty First Century Survival Guide for Kids

Goal Getting: The Science of Achieving Goals

Improve Your Memory Your Thinking and Your Life

Dangerous Beauty: Cosmetics and Personal Care Products

My Dog Eats Better Than Your Kids

Why Busy People Die Young (out 2009)

Available at www.drdingle.com

CDs by Dr D.

"Sick Homes" (double CD, 100 minutes)

"Dangerous Beauty: Cosmetics and Personal Care Products" (60 minutes)

Enquiries and orders:

Email p.dingle@murdoch.edu.au
Mail   Dingle Presentations. Lilly St Studios
13 Lilly St South Fremantle WA 6162
www.drdingle.com

Dingle Presentations Book Order Form
ABN 13347500969

Books	Qty	R retail $	Price
My Dog Eats Better Than Your Kids		25.00 ea	
Sick Homes. Is your home making you sick? (the book)		25.00 ea.	
Dangerous Beauty (booklet)		10.00ea.	
Improve your memory your thinking and your life.		20.00 ea	
The DEAL for Happier Healthier Smarter Kids.		25 ea	
Goal Getting. The Science of Achieving Goals by Peter Dingle and Terry Power		20.00 ea	
Compact Discs			
Sick homes 100 minutes double CD		15.00 ea	
Dangerous Beauty 50 min CD		10.00 ea	

Sub total _____

p & h

All prices include GST   _____

total _____

Postage and handling within Australia

1 book $5   2 books $10   3-5 books $13

Payment by: Credit card, Cheque or money order (Dingle Presentations)

Credit card type.   Visa   Mastercard

Credit card number_____Expirey date_____

Name .... Signature......................................

Address...

State... Postcode ....

Phone .... Fax ....

email ....